Hospital Management

Dr. J. THRESA JENIFFER

Dr. A JOSEPH THATHEYUS

Contents

Foreword

The healthcare sector today stands at the confluence of rapid technological advancement, increasing patient expectations, and the pressing need for organizational efficiency. Hospitals are no longer limited to being mere service centers; they are dynamic, multidisciplinary institutions that require strategic administration and structured management. As a result, hospital administration has evolved into a specialized domain—essential not only for healthcare professionals but also for administrators, policymakers, and academic scholars.

This book, structured around five comprehensive units, is a timely and essential academic resource designed to provide a deep and structured understanding of the multifaceted field of hospital management.

The first unit, Overview of Hospital Administration, lays the foundation by explaining the unique characteristics that distinguish hospitals from traditional industries. It addresses core administrative challenges and provides insight into key planning elements, including hospital layout, equipment acquisition, and functional integration.

The second unit, Human Resource Management in Hospitals, delves into the human aspects of healthcare management. From the principles and functions of HRM to manpower planning and the evolving role of HRD managers, this unit presents tools and strategies for effectively managing healthcare personnel—a crucial factor in delivering quality care.

The third unit, Recruitment and Training, focuses on building and sustaining a competent workforce. It covers departmental functions, recruitment strategies, training methodologies, and the importance of leadership development. This unit reflects the need for continuous professional growth and structured evaluation mechanisms in modern hospitals.

The fourth unit, Supportive Services, emphasizes the critical back-end functions that keep a hospital running smoothly. Services such as medical records, CSSD, pharmacy, food, and laundry may not always be visible to patients but are indispensable for ensuring safety, hygiene, and overall patient satisfaction.

The fifth and final unit, Communication and Safety Aspects in Hospitals, explores the mechanisms of effective information flow and institutional safety. It discusses the integration of technologies like telephone systems, ISDN, CCTV, and alarm systems, and reinforces the importance of fire safety and loss prevention through structured safety rules and planning.

This book not only offers theoretical insights but also provides a practical framework through which students, educators, and administrators can understand and apply hospital management principles in real-world scenarios. It is an ideal academic companion for anyone pursuing a career or specialization in healthcare administration.

Dr. J Thresa Jennifer

Associate Professor, St. Joseph's College of Engineering

02/06/2025

Preface

The healthcare sector is a dynamic and essential part of any society, and its efficient administration is crucial for ensuring quality patient care, operational excellence, and institutional sustainability. In the modern context, hospitals are no longer confined to medical treatment alone—they are comprehensive organizations that require precise coordination across planning, personnel, supportive services, communication, and safety. This reality highlights the increasing importance of hospital administration as a structured academic discipline and a professional practice.

This book, **"Hospital Management,"** has been developed to serve as a comprehensive guide for students, educators, healthcare professionals, and administrators who seek to understand the principles and practices behind effective hospital management. It is tailored to match the curriculum and expectations of healthcare administration programs, especially those focusing on foundational knowledge and practical application.

The content is thoughtfully divided into five units:

Unit I: Overview of Hospital Administration introduces the fundamentals, including how hospitals differ from other industries, challenges administrators face, and the core elements of hospital, equipment, and functional planning.

Unit II: Human Resource Management in Hospitals explores the structure and management of human capital, covering HRM principles, the role of HRD managers, and manpower planning.

Unit III: Recruitment and Training deals with hiring processes, training frameworks, evaluation strategies, and leadership development—all essential for sustaining hospital operations through a capable and committed workforce.

Unit IV: Supportive Services focuses on the backbone of hospital operations, such as medical records, sterilization, pharmacy, food services, and laundry. Each plays a vital role in ensuring efficiency and patient satisfaction.

Unit V: Communication and Safety Aspects in Hospitals underscores the importance of structured communication systems and safety protocols, from ISDN lines to CCTV surveillance, fire safety measures, and loss prevention systems.

Throughout the book, special attention has been given to clarity, relevance, and real-world applicability. Diagrams, comparative tables, and examples are used wherever appropriate to enrich understanding. At the end of each unit, review questions and discussion prompts are provided to help readers consolidate their knowledge and reflect critically on key themes.

It is my sincere hope that this book not only equips learners with theoretical insights but also inspires them to implement best practices in their future careers in hospital management. I am grateful to all educators, mentors, and healthcare professionals whose guidance has shaped the development of this resource.

I welcome feedback and suggestions for future editions.

Dr. J Thresa Jennifer   02/06/2025

Acknowledgments

I take this opportunity to express my heartfelt gratitude to St. Joseph's College of Engineering, OMR, Chennai, for providing me with an excellent academic environment and the opportunity to undertake this project. I sincerely thank the Management, Principal, and the Head of the Department of Information Technology for their continuous support, encouragement, and for providing all the necessary facilities required for the successful completion of this work.

I am also grateful to all the faculty members and staff of the Department of Information Technology for their guidance, valuable insights, and consistent support throughout the course of this project. Their academic inputs and encouragement have played a vital role in enriching my knowledge and enhancing the quality of this work.

I would also like to thank my fellow students and friends for their cooperation, motivation, and constructive suggestions during various phases of this academic effort.

Finally, I thank the Almighty for bestowing upon me the strength, health, and determination to complete this work successfully.

Prologue/Introduction

In the tapestry of human welfare, hospitals stand as vital pillars of society—institutions that not only provide healing but also embody hope, safety, and trust. Yet, the ability of a hospital to deliver effective healthcare extends far beyond clinical excellence. It relies equally on meticulous planning, structured systems, empowered personnel, and a seamless blend of communication and technology. In short, it depends on **efficient hospital administration**.

While much attention in the healthcare field is given to doctors, nurses, and paramedical staff, the realm of administration operates quietly behind the scenes—ensuring that resources are allocated judiciously, services run uninterrupted, safety protocols are upheld, and patient experience is prioritized. Hospital administration transforms a building into a care ecosystem, where lives are not just saved, but respected and dignified.

The idea of this book, **"Hospital Management,"** was conceived from a growing need: to provide structured, accessible, and comprehensive learning material that introduces readers to the foundations of managing a modern healthcare institution. Drawing upon academic rigor and practical relevance, this book serves as a stepping stone for aspiring hospital administrators, healthcare managers, public health students, and even medical professionals aiming to understand the operational side of healthcare delivery.

This text is divided into **five carefully curated units**, each designed to address a core pillar of hospital management:

Unit I – Overview of Hospital Administration begins by clearly establishing the fundamental differences between hospitals and industries. It highlights the unique administrative challenges in healthcare—ranging from regulatory compliance and patient confidentiality to the emotional dynamics involved in caregiving. The unit further delves into the structured processes of hospital planning, equipment procurement, and functional space design—elements that shape the daily workflow of clinical and non-clinical teams.

Unit II – Human Resource Management in Hospitals turns attention to the people behind the processes. It introduces students to core HRM principles and functions in the context of healthcare, including recruitment strategies, skill assessment, the role of HRD managers, and workforce planning. This unit emphasizes that healthcare is a human-centered industry, and its success is dependent on the motivation, training, and retention of its personnel.

Unit III – Recruitment and Training explores the lifecycle of building and nurturing a competent healthcare workforce. It explains how hospitals attract the right talent, the selection process, induction procedures, and the various training methodologies employed to keep staff updated with clinical protocols, behavioral competencies, and ethical conduct. This unit also discusses leadership development and succession planning—essentials in any evolving healthcare organization.

Unit IV – Supportive Services brings to light the operational departments that, while not always patient-facing, play an essential role in hospital performance and hygiene. From Medical Records and CSSD to Pharmacy, Food Services, and Laundry, each sub-system is explored with an understanding of its contribution to patient care and hospital efficiency. This unit demonstrates how logistics and operational services directly affect the overall experience of patients and caregivers.

Unit V – Communication and Safety Aspects in Hospitals addresses two pillars that have become increasingly critical in modern-day hospital management: seamless communication and robust safety infrastructure. It presents technologies such as ISDN, public address systems, CCTV, and alarm mechanisms, while also outlining the fire safety protocols, loss prevention methods, and staff preparedness systems that form a hospital's protective backbone.

Together, these five units do more than impart knowledge—they invite critical thinking, encourage problem-solving, and aim to cultivate a generation of healthcare administrators who are both technically proficient and ethically grounded.

What sets this book apart is its blend of **academic structure with real-world insights**. Concepts are explained clearly and supported with examples, process diagrams, case-based questions, and reflective activities. The book aims to be not just a theoretical guide but a **practical resource**—useful in classrooms, hospital training centers, and academic discussions alike.

As the author, I bring to this work a combination of academic background, research experience, and engagement with hospital-based initiatives and administrative events. My interactions with faculty, industry experts, and student communities have strongly influenced the approach of this book: grounded in curriculum, yet focused on developing competency for real-world challenges.

In closing, I hope this book serves not only as a syllabus companion but also as an inspiration for readers to pursue excellence in healthcare administration. As hospitals continue to evolve, the demand for visionary, skilled, and compassionate administrators will grow. May this book help lay the foundation for that journey.

Dr. J Thresa Jennifer

1. Overview of Hospital Administration

Introduction to Hospital Administration

Hospital Administration is the branch of management that deals with the organization, coordination, control, and overall supervision of healthcare institutions such as hospitals, clinics, and health centers. It involves applying principles of management, leadership, and administration to ensure that healthcare services are delivered efficiently, effectively, and ethically to patients.

In today's rapidly evolving healthcare landscape, hospitals are not merely treatment centers but complex organizations involving multiple departments, technologies, professionals, and regulatory frameworks. Hospital administrators play a pivotal role in integrating clinical services with non-clinical support systems to ensure optimal patient care while maintaining the financial sustainability of the institution.

Key Functions of Hospital Administration:

Planning and Organizing:

Designing hospital infrastructure, resource planning, equipment procurement, and service development.

Strategic and operational planning for short and long-term goals.

Human Resource Management:

Recruiting, training, and managing a multidisciplinary workforce including doctors, nurses, and support staff.

Financial Management:

Budgeting, billing, cost control, and revenue cycle management to ensure financial health.

Operations Management:

Managing day-to-day activities such as admissions, discharge, diagnostic services, and emergency care.

Ensuring smooth coordination among departments.

Quality Assurance and Compliance:

Implementing standards for patient safety, accreditation (e.g., NABH, JCI), and infection control.

Ensuring adherence to legal and ethical healthcare practices.

Technology and Information Systems:

Implementing and managing Electronic Health Records (EHR), telemedicine, and hospital management software.

Ensuring data security and digital transformation.

Patient Relationship and Public Health Management:

Enhancing patient satisfaction through efficient services and grievance redressal mechanisms.

Organizing public health awareness, vaccination drives, and outreach programs.

Importance of Hospital Administration:

Efficiency: Streamlines operations, reduces delays, and improves productivity.

Quality Care: Ensures high standards of clinical services and patient satisfaction.

Regulatory Compliance: Maintains adherence to legal, environmental, and ethical guidelines.

Cost Control: Prevents wastage of resources and optimizes expenditures.

Adaptability: Helps hospitals respond to changing health trends, pandemics, and technology integration.

Overview of Hospital Administration

The hospital is an organization that mobilizes the skills and efforts of widely divergent group of professionals. The main objective of the hospital administration, of course, is to provide adequate care and treatment to its patients. Its principal product is medical, surgical and nursing service to the patient and its central concern is the life and health of the patient.

Distinction Between Hospital and Industry

Hospitals and industries are both large-scale organizations, but they differ significantly in terms of their objectives, operational nature, output, workforce, and societal roles. Understanding these distinctions is crucial for professionals involved in hospital administration, public health, or healthcare policy.

1. Objective

Hospital:
The primary aim is to provide healthcare services, promote health, prevent diseases, and save lives. Profit is not the main motive, especially in public or charitable hospitals.

Industry:
The core objective is to produce goods or services for commercial gain. Industries are driven by market demand and profit generation.

2. Nature of Work

Hospital:
The work involves patient care, diagnosis, treatment, and rehabilitation, requiring compassion and a service mindset.

Industry:
It involves mass production, manufacturing processes, and supply chains aimed at creating marketable products or services.

3. Output

Hospital:
The "output" is measured in health outcomes, patient satisfaction, and quality of care, which are qualitative and patient-specific.

Industry:
Output is typically quantitative, involving measurable units of products or services sold.

4. Workforce Composition

Hospital:
Multidisciplinary professionals such as doctors, nurses, technicians, pharmacists, and administrative staff.

Industry:
Comprises engineers, technicians, laborers, marketing professionals, and production staff.

5. Work Environment

Hospital:
High-stress, emotionally sensitive, requires 24/7 services. Emergency preparedness is critical.

Industry:
Structured, process-driven, often with fixed working hours, focused on efficiency and productivity.

6. Regulation and Ethics

Hospital:
Governed by medical ethics, patient confidentiality, and public health regulations. There is a strong emphasis on ethical care delivery.

Industry:
Governed by business laws, labor laws, environmental norms, and industry standards. Ethics may vary based on the product type.

7. Risk Factors

Hospital:
Risks involve human lives, malpractice, infections, and emergencies like pandemics.

Industry:
Risks may include accidents, machinery failure, and environmental hazards, but not typically human life-critical (unless in hazardous industries).

8. Profit Orientation

Hospital:
Public hospitals are non-profit, while private hospitals may operate on a limited profit basis, prioritizing service quality.

Industry:
Operates primarily for profit maximization, with a clear focus on return on investment (ROI).

9. Technological Use

Hospital:

Uses advanced medical technologies, imaging systems, life support, EMRs, and lab diagnostics.

Industry:

Uses manufacturing technologies, automation, robotics, and supply chain systems.

10. Service vs. Product Orientation

Hospital:

It is service-oriented, where patient experience and personalized care are vital.

Industry:

Primarily product-oriented, with focus on mass production and distribution.

Table1.1 Key differences between Hospital and Industry

Aspect	Hospital	Industry
Objective	Provide health care and improve patient well-being	Manufacture products or provide services for profit
Nature of Service	Human-centric, service-oriented, often lifesaving	Product or service-centric, with commercial intent
Output Measurement	Quality of care, patient outcomes, recovery rates	Quantity and quality of goods or services produced
Regulatory Framework	Governed by health regulations, medical ethics, patient rights	Governed by business, labor, and environmental regulations
Workforce Composition	Multidisciplinary (doctors, nurses, technicians, administrators)	Predominantly technical or labor-based depending on industry
Operational Environment	High emotional stakes, unpredictable workloads	Predictable and schedule-driven production lines
Quality Assurance	Patient safety, hygiene standards, accreditation (e.g., NABH)	Product standards, ISO certifications, quality checks

CHALLENGES IN HOSPITAL ADMINISTRATION

Hospital administration is a multifaceted and ever-evolving discipline that encompasses the management of clinical, operational, financial, technological, legal, and human resource aspects of a healthcare institution. As the complexity of medical services grows with advancements in technology, population dynamics, and patient expectations, hospital administrators face a wide array of challenges that demand strategic foresight, ethical judgment, and adaptive leadership.

1. Human Resource Management

Effective human resource (HR) management is the backbone of a successful healthcare institution. However, hospital administrators face numerous personnel-related challenges:

- Shortage of Skilled Personnel: Many hospitals, especially in rural and underdeveloped areas, struggle to recruit and retain qualified doctors, nurses, and allied healthcare professionals. This leads to increased workloads and compromised patient care.
- Staff Burnout and Attrition: Long working hours, night shifts, high emotional demands, and traumatic patient outcomes often result in professional fatigue, absenteeism, and high turnover rates, particularly in critical care and emergency departments.
- Training and Continuing Education: Medical science and healthcare technologies evolve rapidly. Ensuring that staff stay updated with the latest knowledge through workshops, CME (Continuing Medical Education), and skill-based training is essential but resource-intensive.
- Interpersonal and Interdepartmental Conflicts: Power dynamics between administrative and clinical staff, and poor communication between departments, often lead to disputes and affect organizational efficiency and morale.

2. Financial Constraints

Hospitals must maintain financial sustainability without compromising on quality care—a delicate balance.

- Rising Operational Costs: Expenses related to high-end medical equipment, infrastructure maintenance, and skilled workforce salaries continually increase, especially in tertiary care hospitals.
- Revenue Cycle Management: Balancing revenue generation with patient affordability, particularly in private and not-for-profit hospitals, is a constant struggle. Uncompensated care and delayed payments further affect liquidity.
- Insurance and Reimbursement Delays: Hospitals rely heavily on reimbursements from insurance providers and government health schemes. Procedural delays, claim rejections, and underpayments can severely strain financial resources.
- Budgeting and Cost Control: Allocating funds to different departments while ensuring optimal service delivery, cost-effectiveness, and contingency preparedness requires meticulous planning and audit systems.

3. Technological Challenges

Technology plays a vital role in modern hospital management but comes with its own set of complexities:

- Technology Integration: Implementing systems like Electronic Health Records (EHR), Hospital Information Systems (HIS), and diagnostic automation tools requires significant investment and organizational restructuring.
- Training and User Adoption: Resistance to new technology and lack of IT literacy among medical and paramedical staff can hinder successful implementation.
- Cybersecurity and Data Privacy: Patient data is highly sensitive. Ensuring compliance with data protection regulations (e.g., HIPAA) and preventing cyber threats are critical for institutional trust and legal safety.
- Maintenance and Upgradation: Regular maintenance and timely upgrades of diagnostic tools (MRI, CT, ventilators) are essential to avoid downtime and ensure service quality, which requires dedicated technical teams and budget.

4. Patient Safety and Quality Assurance

Hospitals must consistently deliver safe and high-quality care, which involves:

- Reducing Medical Errors: Preventing misdiagnoses, medication mix-ups, surgical complications, and procedural errors through standardized protocols and checklists.
- Infection Prevention and Control (IPC): Hospital-acquired infections (HAIs) like MRSA or C. difficile pose serious threats. Ensuring robust sanitation, waste management, and sterilization practices is vital.
- Clinical Governance: Establishing systems for continuous monitoring, audit trails, clinical pathways, morbidity & mortality reviews, and patient feedback.
- Accreditation Standards Compliance: Maintaining certifications such as NABH (India), JCI (International), or ISO involves rigorous adherence to protocols and documentation.

5. Infrastructure and Space Management

Physical infrastructure significantly influences patient care and operational flow.

- Overcrowding and Bed Shortage: Particularly in urban public hospitals, this leads to poor patient satisfaction, cross-infections, and staff overload.
- Functional Design and Layout: Optimal space planning for smooth movement of patients, staff, and equipment across various departments—OPD, ER, ICU, OT—is crucial for efficiency and infection control.
- Maintenance and Utilities: Continuous operation of critical systems like HVAC, oxygen lines, elevators, water treatment, and electrical grids is necessary to avoid disruptions.

6. Regulatory and Legal Issues

Hospitals operate in a tightly regulated environment.

- Medical Legal Risks: Increased awareness and consumer rights have led to more lawsuits. Allegations of negligence, documentation lapses, or procedural delays can result in heavy penalties and reputational damage.
- Licensing and Statutory Compliance: Hospitals must secure and renew numerous licenses (e.g., for radiology, pharmacy, biomedical waste) and adhere to fire, building, and environmental norms.
- Dynamic Policy Environment: Changing tax norms (e.g., GST), drug pricing regulations, and insurance coverage criteria require constant adaptation of hospital policies and billing structures.

7. Emergency and Disaster Preparedness

Hospitals must be prepared for unforeseen events that strain capacity and resources.

- Disaster Response Plans: Hospitals need strategic preparedness for natural disasters (earthquakes, floods), pandemics (COVID-19), and mass casualty events.
- Resource Mobilization: Scaling up ICU beds, staffing, and critical supplies on short notice requires agile supply chains and coordination.
- Communication and Command Systems: Establishing robust internal and external communication lines, triage systems, and decision-making hierarchies during crises is essential.

8. Patient-Centric Challenges

Patients are increasingly demanding not just treatment but empathetic, transparent, and personalized care.

- Patient Satisfaction: Long wait times, impolite behavior, lack of information, and inadequate amenities often lead to dissatisfaction despite good clinical outcomes.
- Grievance Handling: Hospitals need formal grievance redressal mechanisms that resolve complaints professionally and feed into quality improvement loops.
- Cultural Competence: In multilingual and diverse societies, hospitals must ensure inclusivity through interpreters, culturally sensitive care, and non-discriminatory practices.

9. Departmental Coordination and Workflow Efficiency

A hospital is a complex system where seamless coordination is critical.

- Interdepartmental Synergy: Smooth handoffs between outpatient, inpatient, diagnostic, pharmacy, and billing units are essential to avoid delays and medical errors.
- Process Standardization: Use of SOPs (Standard Operating Procedures), automation, and workflow optimization tools can minimize inefficiencies and human error.
- Communication Gaps: Lack of real-time information sharing among departments leads to redundancy and patient dissatisfaction.

10. Ethical and Social Responsibilities

Hospitals carry ethical obligations beyond clinical care.

- Ethical Dilemmas: Decision-making in cases involving organ donation, palliative care, resuscitation, or consent must be handled with sensitivity and ethical rigor.
- Public Health Engagement: Hospitals should contribute to community well-being through vaccination drives, screenings, awareness campaigns, and mobile health services.
- Equity and Inclusion: Ensuring that healthcare is accessible to underprivileged and marginalized groups, either through government schemes or internal subsidies, is a moral imperative.

Hospital administrators today must operate in an environment of constant change, uncertainty, and rising expectations. Addressing these challenges requires a blend of clinical insight, business acumen, technological literacy, ethical judgment, and empathetic leadership. Only through holistic, integrated, and adaptive approaches can hospitals thrive as institutions of healing and public trust.

Hospital Planning

Hospital planning is an intricate and multidisciplinary process aimed at designing and developing healthcare facilities that are capable of delivering high-quality, safe, and accessible medical services to the population, both in the present and in the future. It involves not only architectural and engineering aspects but also strategic, operational, financial, legal, environmental, and technological considerations. The objectives of hospital planning go beyond building structures—they aim to ensure the efficient delivery of patient care, optimal utilization of resources, legal compliance, cost-effectiveness, and the creation of a therapeutic environment that enhances patient recovery. A well-planned hospital must also be capable of adapting to changing disease patterns, demographic shifts, and technological innovations.

Hospital planning encompasses various types, starting with strategic planning, which defines the long-term vision and mission of the hospital, identifies target populations, and outlines services like general medicine, specialty clinics, trauma care, and teaching or research facilities. It also considers alignment with national healthcare goals such as universal health coverage, maternal and child health, or digital health transformation. Operational planning addresses workflow efficiency, patient throughput, appointment systems, infection control protocols, clinical pathways, and contingency plans for emergencies. Financial planning involves capital budgeting, operational budgeting, insurance partnerships, donor funding, medical tourism strategies, and cash flow projections. Hospitals must also plan for cost control measures like lean management and equipment leasing options. Manpower planning is critical to determine staffing norms, skill mix, shift rotations, incentive structures, continuing medical education (CME), and workload balancing to avoid staff burnout. Succession planning and human resource forecasting are also part of long-term staff planning.

In terms of infrastructure and layout, planners must consider zoning regulations, fire safety clearances, and environmental sustainability. The layout must allow for expansion, accessibility, departmental adjacency, and efficient movement of patients, staff, and materials. Functional zoning of areas into clean, dirty, sterile, and public spaces minimizes infection risk. Special attention should be given to disaster-resilient design—including seismic proofing, flood management, fire detection systems, and surge capacity for pandemics. Patient-centric design elements such as natural lighting, healing gardens, art therapy spaces, signage in multiple languages, and waiting area comfort enhance the healing experience. Smart hospitals also integrate green building norms (like GRIHA or LEED), use solar power, and install water recycling units.

The planning process starts with community needs assessment, including epidemiological studies, GIS mapping, public health indicators, and feedback from stakeholders like local health officials, NGOs, and citizens. Site selection should consider not only land availability and cost but also proximity to residential areas, public transport, ambulance access, elevation (to avoid flooding), and environmental impact. Capacity planning must reflect the projected disease burden, specialty care needs, demographic growth, and seasonal variations in healthcare demand. Departmental planning involves precise spatial organization—such as having the laboratory near OPD for quick diagnostics, or labor rooms near NICU and operation theatres. Support services like kitchen, laundry, CSSD, blood bank, and medical gas plants must be carefully placed to minimize noise and optimize service access.

Functional flow planning ensures unidirectional movement of patients and supplies, segregation of contaminated and clean zones, and optimal access to elevators and corridors. It must support lean operations with minimal delays, reduced queuing, and efficient service turnaround times. Design principles must incorporate safety, flexibility, accessibility, user-friendliness, and energy efficiency. For instance, vertical circulation through elevators should support emergency transport, while barrier-free design ensures disabled access through ramps, braille signage, and specialized restrooms.

Incorporating technological infrastructure is critical. Hospitals must plan for electronic health records (EHR), picture archiving and communication systems (PACS), remote diagnostics, telemedicine rooms, mobile health apps, and AI-based monitoring tools. Adequate IT infrastructure, server rooms, redundant internet links, and cybersecurity protocols must be integrated into the blueprint. Specialized rooms for robotic surgery, hybrid operating theatres, and advanced imaging must be pre-planned for space, load-bearing, shielding, and HVAC requirements. Biomedical equipment planning includes procurement cycles, lifecycle costing, preventive maintenance, and inventory control systems.

Environmental and waste management planning is another essential component. Hospitals must strictly follow biomedical waste management rules, including waste segregation at source, color-coded bins, incinerator or autoclave placement, and documentation of waste movement. Provisions for rainwater harvesting, energy-efficient HVAC systems, solar panels, green roofs, and noise buffering (especially near ICUs) contribute to environmental sustainability. Utility services like 24/7 power backup with UPS and diesel generators, medical gas pipelines, purified water systems, pneumatic tube systems for sample transport, and HVAC zoning require careful technical integration.

Hospital planning must also account for parking and traffic flow management to avoid congestion, with dedicated spaces for ambulances, staff, visitors, and persons with disabilities. Provision of support services like security systems, CCTV, centralized public address systems, intercoms, and call bell systems ensures safety and communication. Cafeterias, prayer rooms, counseling centers, daycare for staff children, and lounges for duty doctors and nurses improve hospital functionality and staff morale.

Despite best efforts, hospital planning is fraught with challenges such as rising construction and equipment costs, delays in government approvals, changing regulations, opposition from local communities, stakeholder disagreements, and rapid obsolescence of technologies. The integration of various professional inputs—from doctors and administrators to architects and environmental consultants—requires seamless coordination and strong project management skills. Additionally, planners must remain mindful of ethical considerations, such as patient privacy, equitable access, informed consent, and community participation in healthcare design.

Equipment Planning in Hospital Administration

Equipment planning is a critical aspect of hospital administration, directly impacting the quality of patient care, operational efficiency, and financial performance. It involves the systematic selection, acquisition, installation, maintenance, and replacement of medical and non-medical equipment in a healthcare facility.

Key Objectives of Equipment Planning

1. **Patient Safety & Care Quality**: Ensure that the hospital is equipped with up-to-date, functional, and appropriate technology to support diagnostics, treatment, and patient monitoring.
2. **Cost Efficiency**: Optimize capital expenditure and operational costs by avoiding unnecessary purchases and ensuring long-term value.
3. **Regulatory Compliance**: Meet standards set by healthcare authorities (e.g., NABH, JCI) and safety norms (e.g., ISO, BIS, CE marking).
4. **Operational Readiness**: Ensure equipment availability aligns with hospital capacity, clinical workflows, and department-specific needs.

Phases of Equipment Planning

1. **Needs Assessment**
   - Involves consultation with medical and administrative staff.
   - Analyze patient load, services offered, specialty needs, and anticipated growth.
   - Categorize equipment as critical (e.g., ventilators), essential (e.g., ECG machines), or optional.
2. **Budgeting and Cost Estimation**
   - Determine capital cost, installation, consumables, AMC/CMC costs, and life-cycle costs.
   - Align the budget with the hospital's financial strategy and procurement policies.
3. **Specification Development**
   - Define technical and functional specifications in collaboration with clinicians and biomedical engineers.
   - Include power requirements, space needs, software compatibility, and integration potential.
4. **Vendor Selection and Procurement**
   - Use tendering processes, quotations, and comparative analysis.
   - Evaluate vendors based on quality, warranty, service support, training, and cost.

5. **Installation and Commissioning**
   - Coordinate with infrastructure teams to ensure suitable space, power, and environment.
   - Perform quality checks, calibration, and trial runs.
6. **Training and Capacity Building**
   - Train healthcare professionals and technicians on usage, safety protocols, and first-line troubleshooting.
   - Documentation of standard operating procedures (SOPs).
7. **Maintenance and Monitoring**
   - Schedule preventive maintenance, calibrations, and equipment audits.
   - Maintain logs for repairs, breakdowns, and performance.
8. **Replacement and Disposal**
   - Define lifecycle and obsolescence criteria.
   - Ensure eco-friendly disposal or recycling per biomedical waste norms.

Types of Equipment in a Hospital

1. **Medical Equipment**: MRI machines, X-rays, CT scanners, ventilators, surgical instruments, infusion pumps, etc.
2. **Diagnostic Equipment**: Laboratory analyzers, ECG machines, ultrasound units.
3. **Non-medical Equipment**: HVAC systems, elevators, kitchen appliances, IT hardware.
4. **Support Equipment**: Wheelchairs, trolleys, beds, sterilizers.

Challenges in Equipment Planning

- Rapid technological obsolescence.
- Balancing quality and cost under budget constraints.
- Space and infrastructure limitations.
- Coordinating between clinical, administrative, and engineering departments.
- Inadequate maintenance and downtime management.

Best Practices

- **Multidisciplinary Committees**: Involve clinicians, biomedical engineers, administrators, and financial officers.
- **Asset Management Software**: Use digital tools for tracking and planning.
- **Lifecycle Costing Approach**: Look beyond purchase price to include maintenance and decommissioning.
- **Vendor Partnerships**: Establish long-term relationships for better service and upgrades.

Functional Planning in Hospital Administration

Functional planning in hospital administration refers to the systematic process of defining and organizing how different hospital departments and services will operate to meet clinical, administrative, and patient care goals efficiently. It focuses on optimizing workflows, interdepartmental coordination, space utilization, and resource allocation to ensure seamless hospital operations.

Objectives of Functional Planning

1. **Ensure Efficient Workflows**: Design processes that reduce delays, redundancies, and bottlenecks.
2. **Promote Patient-Centered Care**: Improve the patient journey from admission to discharge.
3. **Facilitate Departmental Coordination**: Enable smooth interaction among clinical, diagnostic, and support services.
4. **Optimize Resource Utilization**: Make effective use of space, personnel, equipment, and infrastructure.
5. **Enhance Staff Productivity**: Create a work environment that supports staff efficiency and satisfaction.

Key Components of Functional Planning

1. **Clinical Functionality**
   - Define the services to be provided (e.g., emergency, surgery, ICU, maternity).
   - Plan for required staffing, equipment, and patient flow within departments.
2. **Space Planning**
   - Ensure each department has the right space based on workload and service needs.
   - Design layouts for accessibility, infection control, and future expansion.
3. **Workflow Design**
   - Map patient and staff movement to avoid cross-traffic and delays.
   - Streamline diagnostic and treatment procedures for faster turnaround.
4. **Departmental Relationships**
   - Group related services (e.g., radiology near emergency and surgery).
   - Facilitate quick and easy access between high-interaction units.
5. **Support Services Integration**
   - Plan for logistics like supply chain, housekeeping, linen, food services, and waste management.
   - Ensure support areas are strategically located to serve clinical zones without interfering with patient areas.
6. **Infection Control and Safety**
   - Incorporate zoning, isolation areas, hand-washing stations, and proper ventilation.
   - Plan movement routes for clean vs. contaminated materials.
7. **Information Flow and Technology Integration**
   - Plan for IT infrastructure (e.g., HIS, PACS, EMRs).
   - Enable communication between departments through digital platforms.

Steps in Functional Planning
1. **Needs Assessment**
   - Analyze patient demographics, disease patterns, and service demand.
   - Forecast future requirements based on growth and specialization.
2. **Define Functional Requirements**
   - For each department, define activities, number of staff, equipment needs, and patient load.
   - Identify critical adjacencies (e.g., lab and OPD, ICU and OR).
3. **Develop Functional Relationships and Flow Diagrams**
   - Create diagrams to visualize movement of people, materials, and information.

4. **Space Programming**
   - Translate functions into spatial requirements with size estimates.
   - Prioritize essential vs. optional spaces.
5. **Review and Validation**
   - Conduct stakeholder meetings with clinicians, administrators, architects, and engineers.
   - Modify plans based on feedback and operational constraints.

Example: Functional Planning for an Emergency Department

- **Zones**: Triage, minor injury unit, resuscitation area, observation beds.
- **Adjacency Requirements**: Close to radiology, lab, ICU, and ambulance bay.
- **Workflow**: Entry → Triage → Treatment → Admission/Discharge.
- **Support**: Pharmacy, security, waiting area, isolation room.

Challenges in Functional Planning

Functional planning in hospitals focuses on designing workflows, department layouts, and interdepartmental connectivity to ensure smooth operations and patient-centric care. However, it faces several critical challenges. One of the primary difficulties is predicting future healthcare trends and patient needs, which can be influenced by changing disease patterns, demographic shifts, advancements in treatment protocols, and emerging public health crises. Hospitals must remain agile enough to adapt to rising demand for specialized services, increased outpatient care, or unexpected scenarios like pandemics. Another significant challenge is balancing ideal workflows with architectural limitations. Often, existing site constraints or building codes restrict optimal placement of departments or hinder efficient movement of patients, staff, and supplies. For instance, while it may be ideal to place the ICU near the operation theatre and emergency department, spatial or structural limitations may prevent such alignment, compromising workflow efficiency.

Additionally, ensuring adaptability for future technological advancements is a growing concern. Functional plans must allow for seamless integration of emerging technologies such as robotic surgery, advanced imaging, AI-based monitoring systems, and telemedicine. However, this requires flexible space allocation, scalable IT infrastructure, and planning for upgrades in electrical, data, and HVAC systems—often without disrupting hospital operations. Finally, aligning various stakeholder expectations adds to the complexity. Healthcare administrators, clinicians, architects, engineers, and financial planners may have conflicting priorities. While clinicians may emphasize clinical proximity and patient safety, administrators might focus on cost, compliance, and operational efficiency. Achieving consensus among these diverse groups requires extensive communication, compromise, and often, iterative design revisions. Collectively, these challenges make functional planning a dynamic and critical phase in hospital development that demands foresight, flexibility, and interdisciplinary collaboration.

Benefits of Functional Planning

Functional planning plays a pivotal role in enhancing the overall efficiency and effectiveness of hospital operations. One of the foremost benefits is the reduction in patient waiting and treatment times, achieved by optimizing the layout of departments and streamlining workflows. When diagnostic units, treatment rooms, and support services are logically positioned and easily accessible, patients spend less time navigating the hospital and receive timely care, which significantly boosts satisfaction and outcomes. In addition, functional planning facilitates better coordination between departments by ensuring smooth transitions and communication channels across outpatient, inpatient, emergency, diagnostic, and support services. This integration reduces bottlenecks and redundancies, leading to quicker decision-making and more holistic patient care.

Another crucial advantage is the enhancement of safety and infection control. A well-planned hospital layout includes proper zoning (sterile, semi-sterile, and non-sterile areas), designated routes for waste and biohazard disposal, and the separation of infectious patients, thereby minimizing the risk of cross-contamination. Improved staff productivity and morale also result from functional planning, as ergonomic design, clear workflow paths, and appropriate space allocation reduce physical strain and confusion, allowing healthcare professionals to focus more on patient care rather than navigating inefficiencies. Lastly, it promotes the cost-effective use of space and resources by eliminating underutilized areas, minimizing duplication of services, and ensuring that critical utilities and equipment are optimally distributed. In summary, functional planning not only supports high-quality patient care but also contributes to operational excellence, resource optimization, and staff well-being.

2. Human Resource Management in Hospital

Principles of Human Resource Management (HRM) in Hospital Administration

Human Resource Management (HRM) plays a pivotal role in hospital administration by ensuring that the healthcare workforce is skilled, motivated, and aligned with the goals of the institution. The principles of HRM in hospitals are adapted to meet the unique demands of a healthcare environment, where service quality, patient care, teamwork, and ethics are of paramount importance.

Key Principles of HRM in Hospital Administration

1. **Right Person for the Right Job**

- **Principle**: Recruiting staff based on qualifications, competencies, and suitability for specific roles.
- **Application in Hospitals**: Hiring specialists, nurses, technicians, and administrative personnel with the appropriate medical or technical expertise.

2. **Training and Development**

- **Principle**: Continuous skill enhancement to maintain quality and adapt to technological and procedural changes.
- **Application in Hospitals**:
    - Regular training on medical equipment, infection control, patient safety, and emergency procedures.
    - Workshops for soft skills like communication, empathy, and teamwork.

3. **Motivation and Employee Engagement**

- **Principle**: Encouraging employees through recognition, rewards, and career growth opportunities.
- **Application in Hospitals**:
    - Incentives for outstanding service.
    - Programs for mental health support and work-life balance, especially for frontline workers.

4. **Performance Management**

- **Principle**: Monitoring and evaluating employee performance to ensure accountability and continuous improvement.
- **Application in Hospitals**:
    - Periodic appraisal systems for doctors, nurses, and support staff.
    - Use of KPIs like patient satisfaction, punctuality, and adherence to protocols.

5. **Fair Compensation and Benefits**

- **Principle**: Providing equitable pay and benefits based on skills, roles, and performance.
- **Application in Hospitals**:
    - Structured salary scales, overtime policies, insurance, and pension plans.

     o   Additional allowances for high-risk or emergency duties.

6. Workplace Safety and Health

- **Principle**: Ensuring a safe working environment for all employees.
- **Application in Hospitals**:
  - o Provision of PPE, vaccination, and regular health check-ups.
  - o Compliance with Occupational Safety and Health Administration (OSHA) or local health regulations.

7. Legal and Ethical Compliance

- **Principle**: Adhering to labor laws, medical ethics, and professional conduct.
- **Application in Hospitals**:
  - o Ensuring employee rights, confidentiality, and equal opportunity.
  - o Training on patient rights, consent, and ethical treatment.

8. Employee Relations and Communication

- **Principle**: Maintaining open, transparent, and respectful communication between staff and management.
- **Application in Hospitals**:
  - o Staff meetings, feedback systems, grievance redressal mechanisms.
  - o Promoting a culture of respect and cooperation among departments.

9. Diversity and Inclusion

- **Principle**: Valuing a diverse workforce and ensuring inclusive practices.
- **Application in Hospitals**:
  - o Equal hiring practices regardless of gender, caste, religion, or background.
  - o Sensitization training for cultural competence and inclusivity.

10. Strategic Workforce Planning

- **Principle**: Anticipating future staffing needs and planning accordingly.
- **Application in Hospitals**:
  - o Forecasting needs based on patient load, new services, or expansion.
  - o Succession planning for key roles like department heads.

Functions of Human Resource Management (HRM): A Detailed Discussion

Human Resource Management (HRM) is a strategic and comprehensive approach to managing people within an organization. In any sector, especially in healthcare and hospital administration, HRM functions are crucial for recruiting the right talent, ensuring staff satisfaction, enhancing productivity, and aligning workforce capabilities with organizational goals.

Below are the core functions of HRM, discussed in detail:

1. Human Resource Planning (HRP)

Purpose: Ensures the right number of people with the right skills are available when needed.

- Forecasting manpower needs based on current and future demands.
- Analyzing workforce gaps and planning recruitment or training accordingly.
- In hospitals: Planning for seasonal workloads (e.g., flu season), emergency staff, or new departments.

2. Recruitment and Selection

Purpose: Attracting, shortlisting, and appointing suitable candidates for employment.

- Recruitment: Advertising job openings, campus hiring, job portals.
- Selection: Screening applications, conducting interviews, testing, background verification.
- In hospitals: Hiring doctors, nurses, technicians, administrative staff with the right qualifications and temperament for high-pressure environments.

3. Training and Development

Purpose: Enhancing the skills and knowledge of employees for current and future roles.

- Induction training for new employees.
- Skill-based training (e.g., surgical techniques, software use).
- Leadership development for future managers or department heads.
- In hospitals: Continuous education is essential to stay updated with medical advancements and regulatory changes.

4. Performance Management

Purpose: Monitoring and evaluating employee performance to ensure goals are met.

- Setting clear performance standards and goals.
- Conducting appraisals (monthly, quarterly, or annually).
- Providing constructive feedback and creating improvement plans.
- In hospitals: Using KPIs like patient outcomes, accuracy, timeliness, and patient feedback.

5. Compensation and Benefits Management

Purpose: Ensuring fair and motivating financial and non-financial rewards.

- Designing salary structures, bonuses, and incentive plans.
- Providing benefits like health insurance, pension, leave entitlements, and allowances.
- In hospitals: Offering hazard pay, overtime, or risk-related incentives for frontline workers.

6. Employee Relations

Purpose: Maintaining healthy and productive relationships between management and staff.

- Conflict resolution and grievance redressal.
- Promoting open communication, teamwork, and a positive work environment.
- Ensuring compliance with labor laws and fair treatment.
- In hospitals: Crucial for preventing burnout, reducing turnover, and promoting cooperation among multidisciplinary teams.

7. Health, Safety, and Welfare

Purpose: Ensuring the physical and mental well-being of employees.

- Implementing safety protocols and providing protective gear.
- Organizing wellness programs and mental health support.
- In hospitals: Enforcing infection control, immunizations, and safety drills.

8. Compliance with Labor Laws and Regulations

Purpose: Ensuring HR practices follow national and international laws.

- Adhering to labor standards, equal opportunity, working hours, and wage laws.
- Keeping documentation for audits and legal protection.
- In hospitals: Compliance with health sector-specific regulations like working hours for residents and patient safety standards.

9. Career Planning and Succession Planning

Purpose: Helping employees grow professionally and preparing for leadership transitions.

- Identifying career paths and providing opportunities for advancement.
- Succession planning for key roles to avoid leadership gaps.
- In hospitals: Essential for roles like Chief Medical Officer, Nursing Superintendent, or Department Heads.

10. HR Information Systems (HRIS)

Purpose: Using technology to streamline HR activities.

- Maintaining digital records of employee data, payroll, attendance, leave, and training.
- Automating routine tasks and generating analytical reports.
- In hospitals: Integration with hospital information systems (HIS) to coordinate schedules and manage credentials.

Profile of an HRD Manager in Hospital Administration

The Human Resource Development (HRD) Manager in hospital administration plays a vital role in ensuring that the hospital's workforce is competent, motivated, and aligned with organizational goals. Unlike traditional HR managers, an HRD manager focuses on the growth, development, and performance enhancement of the healthcare workforce through training, talent development, and strategic human capital planning.

Key Responsibilities

1. Strategic HR Planning

- Analyze current and future human resource needs.
- Align HRD strategies with hospital goals (e.g., quality patient care, efficiency, accreditation).
- Forecast workforce requirements based on service expansion or technological changes.

2. Training and Development

- Design and implement training programs for doctors, nurses, technicians, and admin staff.
- Organize CME (Continuing Medical Education), skill enhancement, and certification programs.
- Develop orientation and induction programs for new recruits.

3. Performance Management

- Set up appraisal systems based on KPIs like patient satisfaction, treatment accuracy, and adherence to SOPs.
- Identify skill gaps and plan performance improvement programs.
- Coach supervisors and department heads in performance evaluation techniques.

4. Career Development and Succession Planning

- Identify high-potential employees for leadership roles.
- Create structured career pathways and promotion policies.
- Ensure continuity in leadership for critical hospital functions.

5. Employee Engagement and Motivation

- Implement employee welfare initiatives, feedback mechanisms, and recognition programs.
- Conduct employee satisfaction surveys and act on findings.
- Promote a positive work culture and staff morale, especially during high-pressure periods.

6. Change Management

- Lead staff adaptation during hospital upgrades, digital transitions (e.g., EMR systems), or policy changes.
- Facilitate training during mergers, accreditation processes (NABH, JCI), or operational restructuring.

7. Compliance and Policy Formulation

- Develop HR policies adhering to labor laws, ethical standards, and hospital bylaws.

- Ensure compliance with statutory regulations related to health workers.

Essential Skills and Competencies

Skill	Description
Leadership	Ability to lead HRD initiatives across diverse departments.
Communication	Strong written and verbal skills for interaction with all levels of staff.
Analytical Thinking	Use of data to assess training needs, evaluate outcomes, and forecast workforce trends.
Empathy and Emotional Intelligence	Understand the mental and emotional demands on healthcare workers.
Problem-Solving	Address conflicts, performance issues, and resource constraints effectively.
Tech Savvy	Familiar with HRIS systems, e-learning platforms, and hospital management software.

Educational Qualifications and Experience

- Educational Background:
    o Master's degree in Human Resource Management, Hospital Administration, or MBA (HR).
    o Additional certification in Healthcare Management or Training & Development is advantageous.
- Experience:
    o 5–10 years in HR roles, preferably in healthcare settings.
    o Experience with hospital accreditation, compliance, and staff development programs.

Work Environment and Reporting Structure

- Reports to: Hospital Administrator, Medical Director, or CEO.
- Collaborates with:
    o Department Heads (Medical, Nursing, Support Services)
    o Training Coordinators
    o Compliance Officers

Contribution to Hospital Goals

- Improved patient satisfaction through better-trained staff.
- Enhanced employee retention and morale.
- Smoother workflow and interdepartmental cooperation.
- Successful accreditation and compliance adherence.
- Creation of a learning organization culture.

Human Resource Inventory in Hospital Administration

Human Resource Inventory (HRI), also known as **Human Resource Audit** or **Manpower Inventory**, is a systematic process of collecting, analyzing, and maintaining information about all employees in a hospital. It helps hospital administrators to assess the availability, skills, qualifications, and experience of the workforce and to plan for current and future staffing needs.

Human Resource Inventory is a database or record that contains detailed information about each employee in an organization — including their personal data, educational qualifications, work experience, job performance, training history, and other professional credentials.

Importance of HRI in Hospital Administration

1. **Effective Workforce Planning**
   o Helps in determining if the hospital has sufficient staff to meet current and future demands.
2. **Efficient Deployment**
   o Ensures the right person is assigned to the right role based on qualifications and experience.
3. **Succession Planning**
   o Identifies internal talent for promotion or key leadership roles in clinical and administrative departments.
4. **Training Needs Identification**
   o Highlights skill gaps and training requirements across departments.
5. **Regulatory Compliance**
   o Ensures that staff credentials and certifications are up-to-date (important for audits and accreditations like NABH, JCI).
6. **Crisis and Emergency Management**
   o During pandemics or disasters, helps in mobilizing or reallocating resources quickly.

Components of a Human Resource Inventory

Category	Details Maintained
Personal Information	Name, age, gender, contact info, ID proofs
Educational Qualifications	Degrees, diplomas, certifications
Professional Experience	Job titles, previous roles, years of experience

Category	Details Maintained
Current Role Details	Department, shift, responsibilities, supervisor
Skills and Competencies	Clinical skills, technical skills, language proficiency
Training Records	Workshops attended, CME hours, safety training
Performance Records	Appraisals, feedback, disciplinary actions
Licensing and Certifications	Medical registration, nursing license, renewals
Leave and Attendance	Vacation days, sick leaves, attendance patterns
Retirement and Succession Info	Date of joining, retirement plans, replacements

How It Is Maintained

- **Manual Records** (limited and outdated).
- **Spreadsheets or Databases** (common in smaller hospitals).
- **HRIS (Human Resource Information System)**:
  - A digital system integrated with hospital software to manage records, payroll, appraisals, and schedules.

Steps in Creating a Human Resource Inventory

1. **Data Collection**
   - Gather information from employees, departments, and previous HR records.
2. **Data Entry and Organization**
   - Enter data into the HRIS or digital database under relevant categories.
3. **Verification and Validation**
   - Cross-check documents, certificates, and licenses for accuracy.
4. **Regular Updating**
   - Keep the inventory updated with transfers, new hires, training, or exits.
5. **Analysis and Reporting**
   - Generate reports to support HR planning, audits, and policy development.

Applications in Hospital Administration

Application	Use
Recruitment	Identifies vacancies and required qualifications
Training	Detects which departments need skill upgrades
Workload Analysis	Checks staff-to-patient ratios

Application	Use
Compliance & Accreditation	Ensures staff meets licensing requirements
Emergency Planning	Tracks available on-call staff and backups

Challenges in Maintaining HRI

- Data inconsistency or outdated information.
- Resistance from staff in sharing complete details.
- Lack of integration between HR and clinical systems.
- Need for frequent updates due to high attrition in healthcare.

Manpower Planning in Hospital Administration

Manpower planning, also known as Human Resource Planning (HRP), is a critical process in hospital administration that involves ensuring the right number of healthcare professionals with the right skills are available at the right time to deliver quality patient care. In a hospital setting, where efficiency, safety, and 24/7 availability are crucial, manpower planning plays a central role in operational effectiveness.

Manpower planning is the process of forecasting an organization's future human resource needs and developing strategies to meet those needs through recruitment, training, deployment, and retention.

Objectives of Manpower Planning in Hospitals

1. **Ensure adequate staffing** to handle patient load effectively.
2. **Avoid overstaffing or understaffing**, both of which can impact service quality and costs.
3. **Improve patient care outcomes** through optimal deployment of skilled staff.
4. **Support strategic goals** such as expansion, new service lines, or accreditation.
5. **Prepare for emergencies or surges** (e.g., epidemics, disasters).
6. **Identify training needs** to upgrade skills or bridge competency gaps.

Steps in Manpower Planning Process

1. Analyzing Organizational Goals

- Understand hospital vision, upcoming projects, and service demands (e.g., ICU expansion, telemedicine).

2. Assessing Current Manpower

- Conduct a **human resource inventory**: Number of doctors, nurses, lab technicians, admin staff, etc.
- Evaluate current skills, qualifications, and performance.

3. Forecasting Future Needs

- Predict manpower needs based on:
  - Patient admission trends
  - New medical services or departments
  - Retirement or resignation projections
  - Regulatory requirements (e.g., nurse-patient ratio)

4. Identifying Gaps

- Compare current availability with future requirements.
- Identify shortages or surpluses in departments like Emergency, OT, or Diagnostics.

5. Developing Action Plans

- **Recruitment** for shortages
- **Training and re-skilling** of existing staff
- **Internal transfers or promotions**
- **Contract or temporary hiring** during peak times

6. Monitoring and Evaluation

- Regularly review staffing levels and adapt the plan based on actual patient volume, staff turnover, or budget constraints.

Manpower Categories in Hospitals

Category	Examples
Medical Staff	Doctors, Surgeons, Specialists
Nursing Staff	RNs, Nurse Practitioners, ICU Nurses
Technical Staff	Lab Technicians, Radiographers, Pharmacists
Administrative Staff	HR, Billing, Receptionists, Records Officers
Support Staff	Housekeeping, Security, Maintenance, Ward Boys

Benefits of Manpower Planning in Hospitals

- **Improves patient care and safety**
- **Controls labor costs** by avoiding overstaffing
- **Ensures timely service** and reduces patient waiting time
- **Enhances staff satisfaction** through proper workload distribution
- **Reduces turnover** and burnout
- **Assures compliance** with healthcare regulations and accreditation norms

Challenges in Hospital Manpower Planning

- High staff turnover and burnout, especially among nurses
- Difficulty in forecasting patient demand accurately
- Shortage of specialized professionals
- Budget constraints affecting hiring or retention
- Shift-based work and 24/7 coverage requirements

Tools and Techniques Used

- **Workload Indicators of Staffing Need (WISN)** – used by WHO
- **Time-motion studies** to analyze staff efficiency
- **Skill mix analysis** – to balance senior and junior staff
- **HR software/HRIS** – for real-time tracking and planning

Manpower planning is essential in hospital administration to maintain a well-functioning, responsive, and patient-centric healthcare environment. By proactively managing human resources, hospitals can not only **optimize costs** and **enhance service delivery** but also ensure the **well-being and effectiveness of their workforce**. Proper manpower planning helps bridge the gap between human capital and healthcare excellence.

3. Recruitment and Training

Different Departments of a Hospital with Respect to Recruitment

Recruitment in hospitals is a complex and strategic function, as it involves hiring professionals across **multiple departments**, each with **unique skill sets, qualifications, and responsibilities**. A hospital's smooth functioning depends on the timely and accurate recruitment of personnel in clinical, administrative, and support departments.

Below is a detailed overview of **major hospital departments** with their **recruitment considerations**:

1. Medical Department

Staff Recruited:

- **Physicians (General & Specialists)**
- **Surgeons**
- **Anesthesiologists**
- **Pediatricians**
- **Radiologists**
- **Emergency Doctors**

Recruitment Considerations:

- **Educational qualifications (MBBS, MD, MS, etc.)**
- **Medical registration/license**
- **Experience in clinical care or surgical procedures**
- **Specialization relevance to hospital services**
- **Availability for shifts and emergency duty**

2. Nursing Department

Staff Recruited:

- **Registered Nurses (RNs)**
- **Nurse Practitioners**
- **ICU Nurses**
- **Operation Theatre Nurses**
- **Ward and OPD Nurses**

Recruitment Considerations:

- **GNM/B.Sc/M.Sc in Nursing**
- **Nursing Council registration**
- **Clinical experience, especially in critical care**
- **Shift flexibility and emotional resilience**
- **Communication and empathy skills**

3. Paramedical and Allied Health Department

Staff Recruited:

- **Lab Technicians**
- **Radiology Technicians**
- **Physiotherapists**
- **Pharmacists**
- **Dialysis Technicians**
- **ECG/X-ray Operators**

Recruitment Considerations:

- **Diploma or degree in respective allied health sciences**
- **Certification/licensing where applicable**
- **Technical proficiency and accuracy**
- **Familiarity with medical equipment and safety standards**

4. Administrative Department

Staff Recruited:

- **HR Managers**
- **Hospital Administrators**
- **Finance Officers**
- **Billing Executives**
- **Front Office/Receptionists**
- **Medical Record Officers**

Recruitment Considerations:

- **Qualifications in hospital administration, management, commerce, or HR**
- **Experience with hospital systems like HIS, EMR**
- **Communication and organizational skills**
- **Familiarity with insurance and billing practices**

5. Housekeeping and Facility Management

Staff Recruited:

- **Housekeeping Staff**
- **Sanitation Workers**
- **Maintenance Technicians**
- **Laundry Staff**
- **Waste Management Personnel**

Recruitment Considerations:

- **Physical fitness and ability to work in a healthcare environment**
- **Basic hygiene and safety awareness**
- **Prior experience preferred but not mandatory**

- **Willingness to follow infection control procedures**

6. Security Department

Staff Recruited:

- **Security Guards**
- **CCTV Operators**
- **Gate Supervisors**

Recruitment Considerations:

- **Physical strength and alertness**
- **Experience in security services**
- **Ability to manage patient/visitor flow and emergencies**
- **Background verification**

7. Support Services (Catering, Transport, etc.)

Staff Recruited:

- **Cooks and Kitchen Assistants**
- **Ambulance Drivers**
- **Transport Staff (porters, stretcher-bearers)**

Recruitment Considerations:

- **Basic qualifications and relevant skills**
- **Valid driving license for drivers**
- **Understanding of hygiene and dietary requirements**
- **Reliability and time management**

8. Information Technology (IT) Department

Staff Recruited:

- **IT Support Engineers**
- **Network Administrators**
- **HIS/EMR Software Specialists**
- **Data Analysts**

Recruitment Considerations:

- **Degrees in IT, computer science, or related fields**
- **Familiarity with hospital software systems**
- **Problem-solving ability and 24/7 availability for system issues**

Recruitment Strategy Across Departments

- Job Descriptions **must be tailored to the specific role and department.**
- Screening **may include written tests, practical skill demonstrations, and interviews.**

- Credential Verification **is critical in healthcare (medical council registration, certificates).**
- Background Checks **are essential for patient safety and trust.**
- Onboarding **involves orientation programs specific to department protocols (especially in critical care, OT, and emergency).**

Recruitment, Selection, Training Guidelines

Efficient human resource management is crucial for the functioning of any hospital. The recruitment, selection, and training processes must be designed carefully to ensure that the right individuals are hired and continuously developed to meet the healthcare standards, ensure patient safety, and promote a high-quality work environment.

1. Recruitment in Hospitals

Definition:

Recruitment is the process of attracting, identifying, and encouraging qualified candidates to apply for jobs within the hospital.

Objectives:

- **Fill manpower gaps**
- **Maintain quality of care**
- **Address workforce turnover**
- **Comply with medical staffing standards**

Sources of Recruitment:

Internal Sources	External Sources
Promotions	**Job Portals**
Transfers	**Campus Placements**
Re-employment	**Walk-ins**
Employee Referrals	**Recruitment Agencies**
	Social Media/Website

Recruitment Guidelines:

- Prepare accurate job descriptions and specifications.
- Ensure transparency and fairness in the advertisement process.
- Clearly define required qualifications and licenses (e.g., nursing registration).
- Prioritize ethical background and patient-care commitment.
- Use standard application forms and resume formats.

2. Selection in Hospitals

Definition:

Selection is the process of screening, evaluating, and choosing the most suitable candidates from those who have applied.

Selection Steps:

Application Screening:

- Filter based on qualifications, licenses, and experience.

Written Test or Technical Assessment:

- Assess clinical knowledge, technical skills, or aptitude.

Personal Interview:

- Conducted by HR and departmental heads.
- Evaluate communication, problem-solving, emotional stability.

Practical Demonstration/Trial:

- Especially for nurses, technicians, and support staff.

Medical Examination:

- Ensure physical and mental fitness for duty.

Background Verification:

- Check previous employment, criminal records, and references.

Final Selection & Offer:

- Issue offer letter and terms of employment.

Selection Guidelines:

- Use structured interview formats and standardized rating criteria.
- Involve senior clinical staff for clinical role selection.
- Maintain records of each stage for audit and transparency.
- Prioritize ethical values, teamwork, and patient safety attitudes.
- Follow non-discrimination and equal opportunity principles.

3. Training in Hospitals

Definition:

Training is the organized effort to **upgrade skills, knowledge, and behavior** of hospital employees to perform their duties effectively.

Types of Training:

Type	Purpose
Induction Training	Familiarize new employees with hospital policies and departments
On-the-job Training	Real-time learning while performing tasks
Skill-based Training	Improve clinical or technical procedures (e.g., CPR, IV insertion)
Soft Skills Training	Enhance communication, empathy, teamwork
Emergency Preparedness	Handle disasters, mass casualties, fire safety
Continuing Medical Education (CME)	Keep medical staff updated with new research and guidelines
Compliance Training	NABH, infection control, bio-waste disposal

Training Guidelines:

- Training should be **continuous**, **department-specific**, and **need-based**.
- Maintain **training records** (attendance, assessments, certificates).
- Use **internal and external experts** (e.g., senior doctors, healthcare trainers).
- Evaluate training effectiveness through **feedback and post-training tests**.
- Use simulations, role-plays, and case-based learning for clinical training.
- Ensure training is in line with hospital **accreditation and legal requirements**.

Integration of RST (Recruitment, Selection, Training)

Stage	Goal	Impact on Hospital
Recruitment	Attract right talent	Reduces hiring gaps, improves quality
Selection	Choose best fit	Ensures reliable, skilled, and ethical staff
Training	Develop competencies	Enhances care quality, reduces errors, boosts satisfaction

In hospitals, recruitment, selection, and training are not just HR processes — they are fundamental to delivering safe, timely, and efficient patient care. By implementing structured guidelines and continuously refining these processes, hospital administrators can build a capable, motivated, and future ready workforce that meets both clinical excellence and patient expectations.

Methods of Training

Training in hospital administration is essential to equip healthcare managers, administrative staff, and support teams with the knowledge, skills, and attitude necessary for delivering efficient, patient-centered, and compliant healthcare services. The training methods must be tailored to both clinical and non-clinical environments, balancing operational needs with skill development.

1. On-the-Job Training (OJT)

Description:

Training provided at the workplace while the employee is performing actual tasks under supervision.

Applications:

- Front desk management
- Billing and insurance processing
- Medical records handling
- Use of hospital software (HIS, EMR)

Advantages:

- Real-time learning
- Cost-effective
- Immediate application of skills

2. Classroom (Instructor-Led) Training

Description:

Formal sessions conducted by trainers, HR personnel, or subject matter experts in a dedicated training environment.

Applications:

- Orientation/Induction programs
- Hospital policy briefings
- Compliance with standards (e.g., NABH, JCI)

Advantages:

- Structured learning
- Group discussions and Q&A possible

- Effective for theoretical concepts

3. Simulation-Based Training

Description:

Use of realistic scenarios and environments to mimic real-life challenges.

Applications:

- Emergency response training
- Fire safety drills
- Disaster preparedness
- Handling patient aggression

Advantages:

- Safe environment for practice
- Builds confidence and readiness
- Reduces real-world errors

4. E-Learning and Web-Based Modules

Description:

Online courses and digital learning platforms offering flexibility in training delivery.

Applications:

- Cybersecurity awareness
- Hospital information systems
- Soft skills and language training

Advantages:

- Accessible anytime, anywhere
- Cost-effective for large groups
- Trackable progress and assessments

5. Role-Playing and Case Studies

Description:

Participants act out scenarios or analyze real-world administrative cases.

Applications:

- Conflict resolution
- Ethical decision-making

- Patient interaction scenarios

Advantages:

- Enhances critical thinking
- Improves interpersonal and communication skills
- Encourages empathy and teamwork

6. Mentorship and Coaching

Description:

One-on-one or small group sessions where experienced staff guide less experienced employees.

Applications:

- Leadership development
- Departmental operations
- Long-term performance improvement

Advantages:

- Personalized guidance
- Encourages professional growth
- Builds organizational loyalty

7. Workshops and Seminars

Description:

Short-term training sessions focused on specific administrative topics.

Applications:

- Hospital budgeting
- Quality assurance
- Legal and ethical issues in healthcare

Advantages:

- Interactive and practical
- Knowledge-sharing from experts
- Networking opportunities

8. Cross-Training

Description:

Training employees in multiple roles or departments to improve flexibility.

Applications:

- HR staff learning patient services
- Admins trained in inventory or facility management

Advantages:

- Improves departmental collaboration
- Increases staffing flexibility
- Reduces disruption during absences

9. Continuing Education (CME/CNE)

Description:

Formal ongoing education for professionals to update their knowledge and skills.

Applications:

- Healthcare laws and regulations
- Technology upgrades
- Accreditation standards

Advantages:

- Maintains professional competency
- Required for license renewals
- Enhances service quality

Hospital administrators and staff need multifaceted training methods to function efficiently in today's complex healthcare environment. A blended approach — combining hands-on training, classroom learning, e-learning, and simulation — ensures that both administrative and clinical teams are competent, compliant, and compassionate. Regular and methodical training also enhances hospital reputation, staff morale, and patient satisfaction.

Evaluation of Training in Hospital Administration

Training is a crucial element in hospital administration, but its effectiveness cannot be assumed without proper evaluation. Evaluation of training refers to the systematic process of assessing how well a training program has met its objectives and the extent to which it has improved employee performance and contributed to organizational goals. It ensures that training efforts result in real, measurable outcomes, such as enhanced skills, improved efficiency, and better patient care. The primary objectives of training evaluation are to determine whether training met its goals, assess improvements in knowledge and behavior, justify training costs, and guide future training programs.

In a hospital setting, training evaluation holds immense importance due to its direct impact on patient safety, clinical quality, legal compliance, and staff performance. With increasing complexity in healthcare systems and growing regulatory demands (such as NABH or JCI), evaluating training ensures that hospitals remain compliant and competitive while delivering high-quality patient care. One of the most widely accepted models for training evaluation is Kirkpatrick's Four-Level Model. The first level, Reaction, measures how participants felt about the training—whether they found it useful, engaging, and relevant. This can be assessed through feedback forms or surveys. The second level, Learning, evaluates the increase in knowledge or skills gained, usually through pre- and post-training assessments, quizzes, or demonstrations.

The third level, Behavior, measures whether employees apply what they learned in their actual job roles. This often involves observation, supervisor feedback, or performance reviews. In hospitals, for example, a nurse trained in infection control must demonstrate those practices consistently on the job. The final level, Results, looks at the overall impact of the training on organizational performance. This includes improvements in patient satisfaction, reduced error rates, faster service delivery, or cost reductions. For example, if a training program on safe medication administration leads to a measurable drop in medication errors, it shows success at the results level.

Other models like the Phillips ROI model build upon Kirkpatrick by adding a fifth level that measures the return on investment (ROI) of training. This quantifies the net benefits of training compared to its costs, offering financial justification for the program. Another useful model is the CIPP (Context, Input, Process, Product) Model, which evaluates training based on why it is needed, how it is designed and implemented, and what outcomes it achieves.

Multiple methods can be used to evaluate training. These include surveys, tests, performance observations, interviews, focus groups, and analysis of key performance indicators (KPIs). In hospitals, relevant KPIs might include a reduction in patient complaints, fewer clinical errors, improved audit scores, or shorter patient wait times. Despite its importance, training evaluation faces several challenges. These include time and resource limitations, subjective feedback, difficulty in measuring behavior change, and complexities in data collection. Employees may also be reluctant to provide honest feedback, and the impact of training may take time to materialize.

To overcome these challenges, hospitals should adopt best practices such as setting clear training objectives, using multiple evaluation methods, involving supervisors in follow-up assessments, and aligning training outcomes with organizational goals. Using technology like Learning Management Systems (LMS), dashboards, and online surveys can streamline the evaluation process. A practical example of effective training evaluation could involve a hospital conducting a medication safety training for nurses. If participants report positive feedback (reaction), show improved scores (learning), follow correct medication protocols (behavior), and medication errors decrease (results), the training can be deemed successful.

In conclusion, training evaluation in hospital administration is vital to ensure that training efforts are not wasted and that they lead to tangible improvements in employee competence, patient safety, and operational efficiency. A well-evaluated training program supports strategic decision-making, strengthens regulatory compliance, and builds a culture of continuous learning and accountability in healthcare institutions.

Leadership Grooming and Training in Hospital Administration

Leadership grooming and training have become essential pillars in modern hospital administration due to the increasing complexity of healthcare systems. Hospitals are high-pressure environments that require not only medical excellence but also strong, adaptive leadership to manage people, processes, resources, and patient outcomes effectively. Leaders in healthcare settings must be prepared to make high-stakes decisions, manage cross-functional teams, handle crises, and drive strategic change—all while maintaining compassion and ethical responsibility. Leadership grooming and training help identify potential leaders early and develop them through structured programs to meet these challenges.

`1. Concept of Leadership Grooming in Hospitals

Leadership grooming is the process of identifying, nurturing, and preparing potential employees or junior leaders to take on higher leadership roles. In hospital administration, this involves shaping individuals who can lead multidisciplinary teams, coordinate between departments, implement healthcare policies, and manage hospital operations efficiently.

Key Elements:

- **Talent Identification**: Spotting high-potential individuals based on performance, emotional intelligence, communication skills, and decision-making ability.
- **Mentoring and Coaching**: Assigning experienced mentors (such as senior doctors or administrators) to guide, counsel, and monitor progress.
- **Exposure to Leadership Roles**: Delegating responsibilities such as team supervision, task force leadership, or participation in strategic planning.
- **Continuous Feedback and Evaluation**: Providing structured feedback to refine leadership qualities and address developmental needs.

Importance:

- Ensures **succession planning** and continuity in leadership.
- Promotes **employee retention** by offering growth opportunities.
- Develops a pool of **internal candidates** for future vacancies.
- Aligns individual growth with **organizational goals**.

2. Leadership Training in Hospital Administration

Leadership training refers to formal and informal learning activities designed to improve the leadership capabilities of hospital administrators, department heads, and team leads. It goes beyond technical skills to include soft skills, strategic thinking, and ethical leadership.

Objectives:

- To enhance **managerial competence** in healthcare delivery.
- To prepare leaders to handle **multidisciplinary teams**.
- To improve **communication and conflict resolution**.
- To build resilience and **crisis management skills**.
- To promote **patient-centric care** through inspired leadership.

3. Core Competencies Developed Through Training

a. Strategic Thinking

- Ability to align departmental plans with hospital vision and mission.
- Making data-driven decisions for resource allocation and service improvement.

b. People Management

- Effective delegation, supervision, and motivation of staff.
- Fostering teamwork and interdisciplinary collaboration.

c. Communication Skills

- Handling sensitive patient or family interactions.
- Conducting effective meetings and briefings.

d. Emotional Intelligence

- Managing stress and maintaining empathy under pressure.
- Understanding staff concerns and promoting mental well-being.

e. Ethical and Legal Awareness

- Understanding healthcare ethics, patient rights, and compliance with NABH/JCI standards.

f. Change Management

- Leading technological, procedural, or organizational changes effectively.
- Overcoming resistance to change with stakeholder engagement.

4. Methods of Leadership Training in Hospitals

Method	Description	Example
Workshops/Seminars	Conducted by internal or external experts	Workshop on "Leadership during Healthcare Crisis"
Mentoring Programs	Senior leaders guide juniors through job roles	Nursing superintendent mentoring new charge nurses
Job Rotation	Leaders are moved across departments	Exposure to OPD, IPD, billing, and HR units
Simulation-Based Training	Real-life emergency scenarios simulated	Leadership during code blue or mass casualty event
Online Courses & Certifications	Flexible learning platforms for managers	MOOC on "Healthcare Management"
Case Study Discussions	Analysis of real-life leadership dilemmas	Discussing handling of a medical negligence crisis
Leadership Retreats	Intensive off-site programs	3-day strategic leadership camp for department heads

5. Leadership Development Programs (LDPs)

Many hospitals implement **Leadership Development Programs (LDPs)** that run over several months or even years. These programs are structured to include:

- Induction modules
- Classroom training
- Performance evaluations
- Action learning projects
- Team-building activities

Some hospitals partner with academic institutions to conduct certified leadership courses, including topics like hospital finance, quality control, and healthcare IT systems.

6. Relevance of Leadership Training to Hospital Operations

a. Improved Patient Care

Well-trained leaders ensure protocols are followed, patient feedback is acted upon, and care quality improves.

b. Operational Efficiency

Leaders streamline workflows, minimize delays, and reduce resource wastage.

c. Crisis Preparedness

Trained leaders perform better during pandemics, natural disasters, or medical emergencies.

d. Employee Morale and Retention

Good leadership motivates staff, reduces turnover, and builds a positive work culture.

e. Regulatory Compliance

Leaders ensure adherence to accreditation requirements and legal obligations.

7. Challenges in Leadership Grooming and Training

- **Time Constraints**: Hospital staff often work long shifts, leaving little time for training.
- **Budget Limitations**: Leadership training can be resource-intensive.
- **Resistance to Change**: Some senior professionals may resist grooming younger employees.
- **Lack of Structured Programs**: Not all hospitals have well-defined grooming paths.
- **Shortage of Trainers**: Lack of qualified leadership coaches in the healthcare sector.

8. Recommendations for Effective Leadership Development

1. **Integrate training into the hospital's strategic plan.**
2. **Use performance appraisals to identify future leaders.**
3. **Adopt blended learning methods (offline + online).**
4. **Encourage cross-functional collaboration.**
5. **Include soft skills and ethics in the curriculum.**
6. **Partner with external institutes for executive education.**

9. Real-Life Example

A leading tertiary care hospital in Chennai implemented a 6-month leadership development program for charge nurses. Through mentoring, simulation training, and policy workshops, participants were trained to lead units independently. As a result, internal promotions increased by 40%, and patient satisfaction scores improved by 15% within a year. Such examples showcase how structured grooming leads to measurable outcomes.

Leadership grooming and training are not optional but essential for modern hospital administration. The success of a hospital depends as much on its administrators and managers as it does on its doctors and nurses. Effective leaders drive excellence in patient care, staff performance, and operational efficiency. By investing in leadership development, hospitals ensure long-term stability, compliance with regulations, and continuous improvement in healthcare delivery. Future-ready hospitals must prioritize leadership as a core pillar of strategic human resource management.

Promotion in Hospital Administration

Promotion in hospital administration is a crucial component of human resource management that ensures the right individuals are advanced to higher positions of responsibility within the healthcare organizational structure. In the context of hospitals, where efficient administration directly impacts the quality of patient care, timely and appropriate promotion is not only a reward for performance but also a strategic tool for ensuring leadership continuity, employee satisfaction, and institutional growth.

At its core, promotion involves the elevation of an employee from one position to another, usually with increased responsibilities, better status, and improved remuneration. In hospital settings, this could mean advancing a nurse to a supervisory role, promoting an administrative officer to an operations manager, or elevating a junior doctor to a senior consultant position. These role advancements are vital as they enable the institution to recognize and utilize the experience, dedication, and potential of its staff while simultaneously preparing for future organizational needs.

The primary objectives of implementing a structured promotion policy in hospital administration include recognizing and rewarding employee contributions, fostering employee retention, encouraging professional development, and filling higher-level vacancies internally through skilled and experienced staff. Promotions also act as a morale booster, enhancing motivation and job satisfaction, thereby leading to improved performance. Moreover, by promoting deserving employees from within, hospitals can cultivate a loyal and well-trained workforce familiar with institutional protocols and values.

Promotions in hospitals can be categorized into different types. **Vertical promotion** refers to upward movement to a higher rank, usually accompanied by a significant increase in responsibility, authority, and salary. This is the most common and desirable type of promotion. **Horizontal promotion**, on the other hand, involves a change in role or function without much change in pay or status. For instance, a nurse may be moved from general wards to a specialized unit such as ICU or OT, reflecting a shift in responsibilities. **Dry promotions** offer changes in title or authority without corresponding salary increases, often due to budget constraints or policy norms in public sector hospitals. Promotions can also be **open**—where the vacancy is advertised and candidates, both internal and external, compete for the role—or **closed**, where only internal candidates are considered, fostering internal mobility and growth.

The criteria for promotion in hospital administration vary depending on the institution's policies and values. The most commonly used criteria include **seniority-based**, **merit-based**, and **seniority-cum-merit**. In seniority-based promotion, employees are promoted primarily on the basis of the length of service. This approach is simple, objective, and commonly used in government-run hospitals, but may overlook individual performance. Merit-based promotions emphasize the quality of work, skills, qualifications, and contributions to the organization. This method is prevalent in private and corporate hospitals, where performance metrics and appraisal systems play a critical role. The most balanced and widely accepted approach, however, is the **seniority-cum-merit** method, which considers both tenure and performance, thereby ensuring a fair and equitable system.

A well-structured **promotion policy** in hospitals should define eligibility conditions such as educational qualifications, required experience, and performance standards. The process typically involves identifying vacancies, assessing eligible candidates based on performance appraisals and feedback from supervisors, and conducting interviews or evaluations by a promotion committee. The final selection is approved by top management, and the promoted employee is officially informed of the new role, often accompanied by an orientation or induction into new responsibilities.

Promotion in hospital administration serves multiple strategic purposes beyond individual recognition. It helps hospitals retain competent staff, reduce turnover, and build a sustainable leadership pipeline. It also plays a critical role in **succession planning**, especially for key positions such as hospital superintendents, department heads, and nursing administrators. By preparing and promoting capable staff internally, hospitals can ensure that leadership roles are never left vacant, thereby maintaining service continuity and operational efficiency.

However, the promotion process is not without its challenges. One of the major issues is **subjectivity** in performance assessments, which can lead to favoritism or bias. The absence of a structured career path in some hospitals may also demotivate staff. **Lack of transparency**, **inadequate communication**, and **insufficient documentation** can create mistrust among employees. Moreover, promoting individuals without equipping them with the necessary skills for their new roles can lead to underperformance, especially in leadership positions that require training in management, decision-making, and conflict resolution.

To overcome these issues, hospitals must implement fair and consistent **promotion practices**. Performance management systems should be robust and based on well-defined key performance indicators (KPIs). Training programs should be provided to prepare staff for leadership roles before promotion, ensuring a smooth transition. Promotion decisions must be transparent and well-documented, with clearly communicated policies that include grievance redressal mechanisms in case of disputes. In addition, regular audits of promotion processes can help identify and rectify any inconsistencies or biases.

The **importance of a fair and transparent promotion system** cannot be overstated in hospital administration. When employees are confident that promotions are awarded based on merit and performance, they are more likely to be engaged, motivated, and loyal to the organization. This results in better teamwork, improved service delivery, and a positive institutional culture. In contrast, perceptions of unfairness can lead to dissatisfaction, internal conflicts, and even attrition of skilled staff.

A real-world example would be a multi-specialty hospital that implemented an internal leadership development program for mid-level administrators. Employees were evaluated on their performance, leadership potential, and willingness to take on additional responsibilities. The selected individuals underwent structured training, and many were promoted to departmental leadership roles over time. This initiative not only enhanced administrative capacity but also significantly reduced recruitment costs and improved employee retention.

Promotion must also be clearly distinguished from **transfer** and **upgradation**. While promotion involves a rise in hierarchy, transfer usually means a shift to a different role or location at the same level, and upgradation refers to a salary or status increase without necessarily changing job duties. These distinctions are important in managing employee expectations and maintaining operational clarity.

Lastly, promotion in hospital administration must adhere to **legal and regulatory frameworks**. It should be free from any discrimination based on gender, caste, religion, or disability. It should also comply with guidelines from medical and nursing councils, accreditation bodies like NABH or JCI, and labor laws. Fair promotion practices not only fulfill legal obligations but also enhance the hospital's credibility and reputation.

In conclusion, promotion in hospital administration is an essential HR practice that fosters growth, improves morale, and enhances the overall efficiency of the institution. A fair, well-documented, and performance-based promotion policy supports staff development, ensures leadership readiness, and aligns individual goals with organizational objectives. In a sector as sensitive and service-driven as healthcare, strategic promotion is key to nurturing talent, retaining professionals, and ultimately delivering high-quality patient care.

Transfer and Transfer Policy in Hospital Administration

In hospital administration, transfer refers to the movement of an employee from one position, department, unit, or geographical location to another within the same organization, without any significant change in their status, pay scale, or job rank. Unlike promotions which involve upward movement in the organizational hierarchy, transfers are typically lateral shifts. They are a vital part of workforce management in healthcare institutions, helping to ensure optimal staff utilization, maintain service continuity, balance workloads, and address individual or organizational needs.

Transfers can occur for a variety of reasons. Administrative transfers are done at the discretion of the management to meet organizational needs—for instance, to fill vacancies in understaffed departments, address service demands in critical care units, or respond to shifting patient loads. Personal or compassionate transfers are initiated upon employee request, often due to personal circumstances such as health issues, family needs, or relocation requirements. Disciplinary transfers may be used as part of corrective action, although such transfers must comply with legal and ethical standards. Mutual transfers, common in large public healthcare systems, occur when two employees agree to exchange posts for mutual convenience. Promotional transfers are also seen, where an individual is transferred to a new department along with an elevation in role.

In hospital environments, transfers help maintain staff flexibility, ensure equitable workload distribution, and reduce employee burnout, especially in high-stress areas like emergency rooms or intensive care units. For example, rotating nurses across departments prevents fatigue from repetitive or overly demanding tasks and broadens their skill sets. Transfers also support institutional expansion by reallocating experienced personnel to newly established departments or satellite facilities.

To manage transfers effectively and fairly, a hospital must have a well-defined transfer policy. This policy outlines the procedures, conditions, and guidelines under which transfers are initiated and implemented. A good transfer policy ensures transparency, prevents arbitrary decisions, and aligns the movement of personnel with both organizational goals and employee welfare. Key elements of a sound transfer policy include eligibility criteria (such as length of service or departmental needs), types of transfers allowed, employee rights, and procedural steps (including documentation, approvals, and notice periods).

One of the primary objectives of a transfer policy is to ensure operational efficiency while maintaining employee morale. It should provide for voluntary transfers while also allowing for necessary managerial discretion in cases of emergency or service disruption. Importantly, the policy should also include a grievance redressal mechanism to address any employee dissatisfaction or disputes arising from transfers. Transparency in communication, equal opportunity, and fair treatment are critical for ensuring trust in the system.

Furthermore, transfer policies should be aligned with labor laws, hospital accreditation standards, and professional council regulations. For instance, transfers of medical staff should not compromise patient safety or continuity of care. Proper handover processes and documentation are necessary to ensure smooth transitions, especially in clinical settings.

To illustrate, a well-structured hospital may adopt a rotational transfer system for nurses, wherein they are systematically moved across departments like general wards, maternity, pediatrics, and ICUs every six months. This approach not only improves their versatility and skill development but also prevents over-dependence on specific personnel in any one unit. Similarly, administrators or technicians may be transferred between departments based on evolving needs such as implementing new health IT systems or managing medical records in newly opened wings.

In conclusion, transfers are a strategic tool in hospital administration that, when managed through a clear and fair policy, contribute to workforce optimization, employee development, and organizational agility. A well-executed transfer policy enhances operational effectiveness, promotes equitable staff distribution, and supports both institutional objectives and employee satisfaction. For hospitals to function smoothly and sustainably, especially in dynamic environments, having a transparent, documented, and responsive transfer policy is not just beneficial—it is essential.

Effective hospital administration relies heavily on the strategic management of human resources across various specialized departments. Each department has unique staffing needs that demand careful planning through systematic recruitment and selection processes to ensure the right mix of skills and competencies. Clear training guidelines and diverse methods of training are essential for enhancing the knowledge and capabilities of healthcare professionals, enabling them to provide quality patient care while adapting to evolving medical technologies and practices.

Evaluating training programs plays a critical role in measuring their effectiveness and identifying areas for improvement, thereby ensuring continuous professional development. Leadership grooming and training prepare individuals to take on greater responsibilities, fostering a culture of strong, visionary leadership that can drive organizational growth and respond efficiently to challenges.

Promotion and transfer policies are vital tools in maintaining workforce motivation, balancing operational needs, and ensuring career progression opportunities. A transparent and fair approach to these HR functions promotes employee satisfaction, loyalty, and retention.

In summary, the integration of sound recruitment, training, evaluation, leadership development, and personnel movement policies forms the backbone of a robust hospital management system. This holistic approach not only enhances individual performance and job satisfaction but also significantly contributes to the overall efficiency, effectiveness, and sustainability of healthcare delivery.

4. Supportive Services

The Medical Records Department

The Medical Records Department (MRD) is one of the most critical supportive services in a hospital, functioning as the central hub for managing patient-related clinical and administrative information. Though it does not directly contribute to patient care like clinical departments, it plays an indispensable role in ensuring that care is well-documented, traceable, and legally compliant. The MRD's functions encompass the collection, organization, coding, storage, retrieval, dissemination, and protection of patient records, making it essential for maintaining the hospital's efficiency, safety, and credibility.

Every time a patient interacts with the hospital—whether for outpatient consultation, inpatient admission, emergency care, surgery, or follow-up—the details are meticulously documented in their medical records. These include case histories, progress notes, diagnostic findings, lab and imaging results, treatment plans, prescriptions, nursing care notes, operative and anesthesia reports, consent forms, discharge summaries, and referral information. The MRD ensures that all of this documentation is collected systematically and stored accurately for future reference, enabling continuity of care and facilitating interdepartmental coordination.

An efficiently run MRD supports clinical decision-making by ensuring that patient data is readily accessible to authorized healthcare providers. This is crucial in emergency cases where immediate access to medical history, allergies, and prior treatments can influence life-saving interventions. Additionally, MRD plays a pivotal role in hospital operations and planning, as the data collected serves as a basis for internal audits, departmental performance reviews, policy development, and healthcare analytics.

In the legal and regulatory context, medical records are considered official documents and may be used in court proceedings, insurance settlements, or medico-legal cases. The MRD ensures compliance with national and international standards such as HIPAA (Health Insurance Portability and Accountability Act), GDPR (General Data Protection Regulation), and other healthcare regulations relevant to privacy, confidentiality, and record retention. Strict protocols are followed to restrict unauthorized access and maintain confidentiality of sensitive patient information.

The department is also responsible for medical coding and classification, using standardized systems such as ICD (International Classification of Diseases) and CPT (Current Procedural Terminology) codes. This aids in clinical research, epidemiological studies, hospital statistics, and insurance claim processing. Accurate coding is essential for billing, reimbursement, and maintaining hospital accreditation under standards set by organizations like NABH (National Accreditation Board for Hospitals) or JCI (Joint Commission International).

With the advent of Electronic Health Records (EHRs) and Hospital Information Systems (HIS), the traditional manual records management has transformed into digital documentation. The MRD now works closely with IT departments to manage, update, and protect electronic records. This digital shift has improved the efficiency of data retrieval, enabled data backup and disaster recovery, and facilitated real-time access to patient records across departments and even remote locations.

Beyond supporting clinicians, the MRD contributes significantly to training, research, and academic activities. Medical students, researchers, and quality control teams frequently rely on anonymized data from medical records to study disease trends, evaluate treatment efficacy, and propose process improvements. The MRD is thus integral not only to the present care but also to shaping the future of healthcare delivery.

Staff working in the MRD typically includes medical record officers, health information managers, data entry operators, and coders. They are trained in medical terminology, data privacy laws, classification systems, and computer applications. Regular training and audits are conducted to keep them updated with evolving standards and technologies.

Moreover, the department plays a vital role in discharge planning by coordinating with various departments to ensure the documentation is complete and accurate before patient discharge. This helps in timely billing, smooth insurance processing, and post-discharge care follow-ups. In case of deaths, births, or surgeries, the MRD also liaises with public health authorities for necessary registrations and certifications.

In summary, the Medical Records Department is the backbone of information management in a hospital. It bridges clinical services with administrative processes, ensuring that patient care is documented, traceable, legally compliant, and useful for future reference. A well-organized MRD enhances hospital functioning in multiple dimensions—clinical, legal, financial, research, and technological—making it an indispensable supportive service in the complex ecosystem of healthcare delivery.

Central Sterilization and Supply Department (CSSD) in Hospital Supportive Services

The Central Sterilization and Supply Department (CSSD) is one of the most essential supportive services in a hospital, dedicated to ensuring the effective cleaning, disinfection, sterilization, storage, and distribution of medical instruments, equipment, and supplies. Though it operates behind the scenes, the CSSD plays a crucial role in patient safety by maintaining a sterile environment and preventing healthcare-associated infections (HAIs), which are among the leading causes of morbidity and mortality in hospital settings.

Core Functions of CSSD

The CSSD is tasked with the decontamination of all reusable instruments and supplies used in surgical, diagnostic, and therapeutic procedures across various departments. These include the operating theatres (OT), labor rooms, intensive care units (ICUs), wards, outpatient departments (OPDs), emergency rooms, and laboratories. The department handles thousands of instruments and kits daily, necessitating high levels of precision, hygiene, and coordination.

The workflow of CSSD typically involves the following stages:

1. Receiving & Decontamination: Used instruments and supplies are received from clinical areas in closed containers. Decontamination begins with manual or automated cleaning, using detergents and enzymatic solutions to remove blood, tissue, and other biological contaminants.
2. Inspection & Assembly: Once cleaned, instruments are inspected for damage or malfunction. They are then assembled into procedural sets based on specific surgical or diagnostic requirements. Proper lubrication (known as milking) of hinged instruments may be carried out to maintain functionality.
3. Packaging: The items are wrapped or sealed in sterilization-compatible materials (e.g., pouches, wraps, containers) and labeled with sterilization indicators and tracking codes.
4. Sterilization: Instruments are sterilized using appropriate methods depending on material type, temperature sensitivity, and intended use:
    o Steam Sterilization (Autoclaving) – Most common; effective for heat-stable items.
    o Ethylene Oxide (ETO) Gas Sterilization – For heat- and moisture-sensitive instruments.
    o Hydrogen Peroxide Plasma – Low-temperature sterilization for delicate items.
    o Dry Heat Sterilization – Used for items that may be damaged by moisture.
    o Chemical Sterilization – For items that cannot withstand high temperatures.
5. Storage: Sterilized instruments are stored in sterile storage areas under controlled environmental conditions (temperature, humidity, airflow). Storage protocols ensure that instruments remain sterile until the point of use.

6. Distribution: Upon request, sterile packs are dispatched to user departments. CSSD staff maintain accurate logs of items sent and received, ensuring accountability and traceability.

Quality Assurance and Monitoring

The CSSD is governed by stringent quality control protocols to ensure that sterilization processes are effective. These include:

- Biological Indicators – Used periodically to test the efficacy of sterilization.
- Chemical Indicators – Attached to packs to confirm exposure to sterilization conditions.
- Mechanical Indicators – Monitor temperature, pressure, and time during sterilization cycles.
- Documentation and Record Keeping – All sterilization cycles are documented with date, time, operator name, load details, and indicator results.

Regular validation and calibration of sterilization equipment are mandatory. Internal audits, infection control reviews, and adherence to global guidelines (e.g., CDC, WHO, AAMI, ISO standards) are part of CSSD's quality assurance system.

Role in Infection Control

CSSD is at the forefront of hospital infection prevention strategies. It ensures that no contaminated instruments are reused, thereby reducing cross-contamination risks. The department works closely with the Infection Control Committee and hospital epidemiologists to report issues, update protocols, and respond to outbreaks. Sterilization failures or breaches are treated with utmost seriousness, often triggering full investigations and corrective action.

Technology and Automation

Modern CSSDs are equipped with automated washer-disinfectors, sterilizers, barcode tracking systems, and computerized inventory management systems. Automation improves accuracy, enhances throughput, and reduces human error. Barcode systems allow real-time tracking of instruments from sterilization to point-of-use, aiding in accountability and efficient recalls if necessary.

With the evolution of Minimally Invasive Surgery (MIS) and advanced diagnostic tools, the CSSD also handles delicate equipment such as endoscopes, fiber optics, robotic surgical tools, and implantable devices. These require specialized cleaning protocols and validation methods.

Human Resource and Training

The effectiveness of the CSSD heavily depends on the skill and vigilance of its personnel. Staff typically include:

- Sterile Processing Technicians
- CSSD Supervisors
- Biomedical Engineers
- Support Workers

They receive rigorous training in:

- Microbiology and infection control
- Instrument handling and classification

- Sterilization technology and protocols
- Equipment maintenance and troubleshooting
- Health and safety regulations

Continuous training is crucial as sterilization standards evolve and new equipment is introduced.

Integration with Other Departments

The CSSD works in close coordination with:

- Operating Theatres – for surgical set preparation and emergency supplies.
- ICUs and Wards – for sterile dressing materials and equipment.
- Pharmacy – in some settings, for sterilizing reusable pharmaceutical tools.
- Biomedical Department – for equipment maintenance and servicing.

The Central Sterilization and Supply Department (CSSD) is not merely a behind-the-scenes function but a core pillar of hospital safety and quality assurance. By ensuring that all instruments and materials are thoroughly sterilized and properly managed, it safeguards both patients and healthcare workers from infection risks. A well-organized, well-staffed, and technologically advanced CSSD is essential for supporting surgical precision, maintaining compliance with medical regulations, and enhancing the overall performance of the hospital. In today's healthcare landscape, where patient safety and infection control are top priorities, the CSSD stands as an indispensable guardian of clinical integrity and care quality.

Role of Pharmacy in Supportive Services of Hospital

The pharmacy is one of the most essential supportive services in a hospital, playing a crucial role in ensuring the safe, effective, and timely delivery of medications to patients. It supports clinical departments by managing the procurement, storage, preparation, dispensing, and monitoring of pharmaceutical products. A hospital pharmacy operates under strict regulatory frameworks and collaborates closely with physicians, nurses, and other healthcare professionals to promote rational drug use, improve therapeutic outcomes, and reduce medication-related errors. It serves both inpatient and outpatient departments and may be divided into sub-units such as inpatient pharmacy, outpatient pharmacy, emergency pharmacy, and clinical pharmacy.

Core Responsibilities of Hospital Pharmacy

Procurement and Inventory Management:

The pharmacy is responsible for sourcing high-quality drugs, surgical items, and consumables from reliable suppliers. Pharmacists ensure the availability of essential, life-saving, and specialty drugs at all times. The procurement process involves evaluating suppliers, negotiating contracts, adhering to hospital budgets, and maintaining adequate stock levels while avoiding overstock or expiry.

Storage and Preservation:

Pharmaceuticals require strict storage conditions to maintain their efficacy. Hospital pharmacies ensure that drugs are stored under appropriate temperature, humidity, and lighting conditions. This includes maintaining cold chains for vaccines, insulin, and other temperature-sensitive drugs. Proper labeling, shelf-life monitoring, and first-expiry-first-out (FEFO) methods are followed to minimize wastage.

Dispensing of Medications:

The pharmacy is responsible for accurately dispensing prescribed medications to both inpatients and outpatients. In inpatient settings, unit-dose systems or ward stock systems are used. Pharmacists cross-check prescriptions for potential drug interactions, dosing errors, contraindications, and allergies, thereby reducing medication errors and improving patient safety.

Clinical Pharmacy Services:

Modern hospital pharmacies increasingly offer clinical pharmacy services, where pharmacists are involved in direct patient care. They participate in ward rounds, provide drug information, monitor drug therapy outcomes, and assist in adverse drug reaction (ADR) reporting. Pharmacists act as medication advisors, helping to optimize drug therapy and promote evidence-based treatment practices.

Formulary Management and Drug Policy:

The pharmacy plays a central role in formulating and maintaining the hospital drug formulary, which is a list of approved medications for use in the hospital. It helps control costs and standardizes treatment protocols. Pharmacists work with the Pharmacy and Therapeutics (P&T) Committee to review new drug requests, evaluate efficacy, safety, and cost-effectiveness, and update prescribing guidelines.

Compounding and Preparation:

In some settings, hospital pharmacists are involved in compounding medications, such as preparing IV admixtures, pediatric doses, ointments, and other non-commercially available drug formulations. They ensure proper dosage accuracy, sterility, and compatibility of compounded products, particularly for chemotherapy, neonatal, or critical care patients.

Emergency Support and Night Services:

Hospital pharmacies provide round-the-clock support, especially during emergencies. The emergency pharmacy ensures that critical drugs like antivenoms, cardiac drugs, and resuscitation medications are available at any hour. This is crucial for trauma care, surgeries, and intensive care units where quick drug availability can be life-saving.

Education and Training:

Pharmacists conduct training programs for nursing staff and interns on safe medication administration, storage of high-risk drugs, and infection control. They also help in educating patients about proper drug usage, possible side effects, and the importance of adherence, especially for chronic conditions like diabetes, hypertension, or tuberculosis.

Research and Pharmacovigilance:

Hospital pharmacies often contribute to clinical research, drug trials, and pharmacovigilance programs. They report adverse drug reactions (ADRs) to regulatory bodies, maintain drug safety records, and help monitor post-marketing surveillance of new medications. This ensures a culture of continuous monitoring and improvement in drug safety.

Regulatory Compliance and Ethical Responsibility:

Hospital pharmacies play a critical role in ensuring the safe, legal, and ethical handling of medications within a healthcare facility. To fulfill this role effectively, they must comply with a wide array of national laws, regulatory guidelines, and institutional protocols. These responsibilities are essential not only for maintaining operational standards but also for safeguarding patient health and public trust.

1. Compliance with National Drug Laws and Regulations

Hospital pharmacies must operate in strict adherence to national drug control laws such as:

- **India**: Drugs and Cosmetics Act, 1940, Narcotic Drugs and Psychotropic Substances Act (NDPS), 1985.
- **United States**: Federal Food, Drug, and Cosmetic Act, Controlled Substances Act enforced by the FDA and DEA.

These laws regulate the manufacture, storage, distribution, and dispensation of pharmaceuticals, ensuring that only approved and safe drugs are provided to patients. Compliance involves maintaining current licenses and ensuring that all pharmaceutical activities meet the criteria laid down by authorities.

2. Licensing and Documentation

Hospital pharmacies must obtain and renew various licenses, such as:

- **Drug sale and storage licenses** (including Schedule X drugs in India).
- **Narcotics handling licenses**, if applicable.
  They must also maintain up-to-date documentation related to procurement, storage, distribution, and use of all medications, particularly controlled and high-risk substances.

3. Management of Narcotic and Controlled Drugs

Special attention is required for handling narcotic and psychotropic drugs due to their potential for abuse and legal implications. Hospital pharmacists are responsible for:

- Accurate inventory and usage records.
- Secure storage in designated locked cabinets.
- Issuance based only on valid prescriptions.
- Periodic audits and reporting to regulatory authorities.

Any discrepancy in narcotics inventory can trigger legal investigations and must be immediately reported.

4. Prescription Audits and Monitoring

Regular audits of prescriptions and medication records help ensure:

- Rational and evidence-based prescribing practices.
- Detection of potential prescription errors, misuse, or overuse.
- Compliance with hospital formulary guidelines and standard treatment protocols.

This function also supports antimicrobial stewardship programs and overall quality control in drug therapy management.

5. Ethical Dispensing Practices

Ethical responsibility in a hospital pharmacy extends beyond legality. Pharmacists must ensure:

- Medications are dispensed only against valid prescriptions.
- Patients receive the correct drug, dose, and instructions.
- No undue influence from pharmaceutical marketing affects dispensing.
- Equitable access to medications without discrimination.

6. Safe Disposal of Expired and Unused Medications

Improper disposal of pharmaceuticals can lead to environmental contamination and potential drug misuse. Hospital pharmacies are responsible for:

- Identifying and segregating expired or unused medications.
- Following biomedical waste management protocols.
- Coordinating with certified disposal agencies for incineration or other safe destruction methods.
- Documenting the disposal process for regulatory verification.

Hospital pharmacies must comply with national drug laws (such as the Drugs and Cosmetics Act in India or FDA regulations in the U.S.), as well as hospital policies. They are responsible for maintaining drug licenses, narcotic records, prescription audits, and ensuring ethical distribution and disposal of expired or unused medications.

Integration with Hospital Departments

Pharmacy services are intricately linked to all clinical departments. For example:

- In surgery, pharmacists ensure availability of anesthetics and antibiotics.
- In ICU, they help manage high-risk medications like vasopressors and sedatives.
- In oncology, pharmacists handle cytotoxic drugs with specialized safety procedures.
- In pediatrics, dosing calculations and compounding are especially sensitive and require pharmaceutical expertise.

This interdepartmental coordination ensures that drug therapy is patient-centered, timely, and cost-effective.

In conclusion, the hospital pharmacy is a cornerstone of supportive healthcare services. While it may not be directly involved in diagnosis or surgery, it plays a central role in patient treatment, safety, and recovery. By managing the availability, quality, and safe use of medicines, the pharmacy ensures that all departments are adequately supported. The evolving role of the pharmacist—from a dispenser to a clinical advisor—reflects the growing importance of pharmacy in modern healthcare. A well-functioning hospital pharmacy contributes significantly to the hospital's mission of delivering safe, effective, and affordable care, making it an indispensable part of the healthcare ecosystem.

Food Services as Supportive Services in Hospital Administration

Food services in hospitals are a vital component of **supportive services**, which complement the core clinical functions. While medical care is at the center of hospital operations, **nutritional care** is equally important in supporting **patient recovery, immunity, and overall well-being**. A well-organized hospital food service system ensures the delivery of **hygienic, nutritious, therapeutic, and culturally appropriate meals** to patients, staff, and sometimes visitors. In hospital administration, the food service department is managed with the same diligence as any clinical unit because of its direct impact on patient health outcomes, satisfaction, and hospital reputation.

1. Importance of Food Services in a Hospital

The role of food in a hospital setting goes beyond mere sustenance. It:

- Aids in the **healing and recovery process**.
- Prevents **complications due to malnutrition** or improper diet.
- Helps in **managing chronic diseases** like diabetes, hypertension, and kidney disorders.
- Contributes to the **psychological comfort** of patients.
- Enhances the **overall hospital experience** and satisfaction.

In some cases, **nutritional therapy** is a primary mode of treatment, such as in cases of digestive disorders, metabolic issues, or malnourishment.

2. Structure and Organization of Hospital Food Services

A hospital food service department is typically headed by a **Dietician or Food Service Manager**, supported by:

- **Clinical Dietitians** – assess patient needs and prescribe therapeutic diets.
- **Catering Managers** – oversee kitchen operations.
- **Chefs and Food Handlers** – prepare meals according to diet plans.
- **Support Staff** – responsible for serving, cleaning, and logistics.

The department works closely with the **medical team**, **nursing staff**, and **infection control unit** to ensure safety and dietary compliance.

3. Functions of Hospital Food Services

A. Diet Planning and Prescription

- Based on doctor's diagnosis and clinical nutrition assessment.
- Types of diets provided:
  - **Therapeutic diets**: low sodium, diabetic, cardiac, renal, high-protein.
  - **Texture-modified diets**: soft, pureed, liquid diets.
  - **Cultural/religious diets**: vegetarian, halal, kosher, etc.
- Continuous monitoring and adjustments are made based on patient condition.

B. Meal Preparation

- Food is prepared under hygienic conditions with medically approved ingredients.
- Specialized diets are cooked in separate areas to prevent cross-contamination.
- Use of **steam cooking**, **controlled temperature ovens**, and **measured recipes** for consistency.

C. Food Safety and Hygiene

- Following **HACCP** (Hazard Analysis and Critical Control Point) principles.
- Staff undergo training in **sanitation, pest control, hand hygiene, and food storage**.

- Strict **personal protective gear** is used during food handling.
- Periodic **microbiological testing** and **kitchen audits** are done.

D. Meal Distribution

- Meals are distributed to patient wards through **central trolleys**, **tray service**, or **unit kitchen systems**.
- Staff ensure correct delivery as per patient diet cards.
- Coordination with nurses to deliver food at appropriate times (e.g., before medication).

E. Monitoring and Feedback

- Monitoring of patient intake and nutrition adequacy.
- Feedback forms are collected to assess:
  - Taste and quality of food.
  - Timeliness of delivery.
  - Patient satisfaction.

4. Special Functions

Emergency and Critical Care Diets

- Nutritional support for **ICU patients**, including **enteral and parenteral nutrition**.
- Tailored meals for **post-operative**, **oncology**, or **pediatric patients**.

Staff and Visitor Cafeterias

- Providing nutritious, affordable meals to doctors, nurses, and administrative staff.
- Maintaining hygiene and quality similar to patient meals.

Training and Continuous Improvement

- Periodic training of kitchen and dietary staff on new diet plans, food allergies, and hygiene protocols.
- Adoption of **modern kitchen technologies** like automated cooking units and temperature-controlled storage.
- Introduction of **green initiatives** such as waste segregation, composting, and biodegradable packaging.

5. Administrative and Managerial Aspects

From a hospital administration point of view, food services are managed like a critical department:

- **Budgeting and Cost Control**: Managing food costs while maintaining nutritional quality.
- **Vendor Management**: Procuring fresh, high-quality raw materials.
- **Quality Assurance**: Standard operating procedures (SOPs) for kitchen hygiene, preparation, and storage.
- **Compliance**: Adhering to national food safety laws (e.g., FSSAI in India).
- **Coordination**: Working with clinical teams for seamless delivery.

6. Challenges in Hospital Food Services

- Ensuring **personalized nutrition** for a large number of patients.
- Managing **diet changes** during emergencies or sudden condition deterioration.
- Balancing **cost and quality** under tight hospital budgets.
- Addressing **cultural preferences** in a diverse patient population.
- Handling **food waste and environmental concerns**.

7. Integration with Other Supportive and Clinical Services

- **With Nursing**: To monitor intake/output and patient satisfaction.
- **With Infection Control**: For hygiene and prevention of food-borne infections.
- **With Biomedical Engineering**: Maintenance of kitchen equipment and storage devices.
- **With Administration**: For audits, budgeting, and overall quality improvement.

In conclusion, the Food Services Department in a hospital plays a central role in the supportive care infrastructure. Its function is not limited to meal provision but extends to therapeutic nutrition, infection prevention, emotional comfort, and overall patient satisfaction. An efficiently managed hospital food service not only contributes to quicker recovery but also enhances the reputation and performance of the hospital as a whole. Administrators must ensure that food services are given due importance in planning, funding, and staffing. As healthcare evolves, nutrition-centric patient care and integrated diet planning are becoming key elements of holistic hospital management. Hence, food services are not just supportive—they are strategic pillars of modern hospital care.

Laundry Services in Hospital Supportive Services

Laundry Services form an indispensable component of the supportive services in hospitals. While often operating behind the scenes, an efficient hospital laundry service is vital for maintaining a clean, safe, and hygienic environment. It ensures the continuous supply of sterilized and sanitized linen for patient care, thereby playing a direct role in infection control, patient comfort, and overall hospital operations. A well-managed laundry service upholds the hospital's commitment to quality healthcare by maintaining high standards of cleanliness and operational efficiency.

Importance of Laundry Services in Hospitals

Hospital linen includes bed sheets, blankets, pillowcases, towels, gowns, surgical drapes, and staff uniforms. These items are exposed to various biological contaminants such as blood, bodily fluids, bacteria, and viruses. Without proper cleaning and disinfection, they can act as vectors for hospital-acquired infections (HAIs), posing a serious threat to both patients and healthcare workers.

Thus, laundry services:

- **Prevent cross-infection and contamination**.
- **Support infection control and hygiene standards**.
- Enhance **patient dignity and comfort** through clean linen.
- Ensure **continuous availability** of linen and uniforms for efficient hospital functioning.

Objectives of Hospital Laundry Services

- To provide **adequate, clean, and disinfected linen** to all hospital departments.

- To manage **collection, segregation, washing, drying, ironing, and distribution** of hospital textiles.
- To ensure compliance with **infection control policies** and **national health guidelines**.
- To reduce **wear and tear** through proper handling and laundering techniques.
- To operate in a **cost-effective and sustainable** manner.

Workflow of Laundry Services

The hospital laundry process generally follows a **closed-loop cycle** involving the following key stages:

1. Collection of Soiled Linen

- Dirty linen is collected from all departments, including wards, ICUs, operating theatres, and outpatient units.
- Linen is categorized as **infected, soiled, or general**, and placed in color-coded bags as per biomedical waste rules.
- Staff use **personal protective equipment (PPE)** during handling.

2. Transportation

- Dedicated trolleys or carts (covered and leak-proof) are used for internal transport.
- Soiled linen is taken through a **separate route** to avoid cross-contamination with clean linen.

3. Sorting and Classification

- At the laundry site, linen is sorted by type, fabric, and level of contamination.
- Heavily soiled or infectious linen is separated for pre-treatment.

4. Washing and Disinfection

- Washing is done in **industrial washing machines** with hot water (60–90°C), detergents, and disinfectants.
- A **two-stage wash cycle** is usually followed: cleaning followed by thermal or chemical disinfection.
- **Enzyme-based** or **oxygen-based** disinfectants are commonly used.

5. Drying and Ironing

- Linen is dried using **tumble dryers** or **sunlight drying areas** depending on resources.
- **Calendering machines** or steam presses are used for ironing and sterilization, especially for surgical linen.

6. Inspection and Repair

- Each item is inspected for tears, damage, or stains.
- Minor repairs are carried out in-house; unfit linen is removed and discarded as per hospital policy.

7. Packing and Storage

- Clean linen is folded, packed, and stored in designated clean areas.
- Special packaging is used for **sterile linen** to be sent to operation theatres or ICUs.

8. Distribution

- Fresh linen is distributed daily or as per schedule to departments.
- A **linen inventory management system** tracks stock, usage, and losses.

Infrastructure and Requirements

- **Laundry Building**: Should be separate from patient care areas and divided into "soiled" and "clean" zones.
- **Machinery**:
  o Washer extractors
  o Hydro extractors
  o Tumble dryers
  o Calendaring machines
  o Steam presses
- **Ventilation and Drainage**: Adequate exhaust systems and water disposal units.
- **Staffing**:
  o Laundry Manager
  o Washmen
  o Sorters
  o Packers and Delivery Staff
  o Maintenance Technicians

Types of Laundry Systems in Hospitals

1. **In-House Laundry**
   o Located within the hospital premises.
   o Complete control over operations, quality, and timelines.
2. **Outsourced Laundry**
   o Laundry is outsourced to an external agency.
   o Reduces capital cost but may risk quality or delay.
3. **Hybrid Model**
   o Certain items (e.g., surgical linen) are handled in-house, while general linen is outsourced.

Linen Management and Inventory Control

Linen management and inventory control are essential components of hospital administration that directly impact hygiene, patient comfort, and operational efficiency. Effective linen management begins with the use of linen registers or specialized Linen Management Software, which help in systematically recording the movement, usage, and stock levels of various linen items such as bed sheets, gowns, towels, and curtains. This digital or manual tracking system ensures transparency, minimizes pilferage, and supports real-time decision-making. To maintain equitable distribution and avoid shortages, linen quotas are allocated to different wards and departments based on their patient load, turnover rate, and specific requirements. This controlled distribution helps in maintaining adequate supply while preventing wastage.

Regular audits are conducted to monitor the condition, availability, and utilization of linen. These audits help identify patterns of overuse, losses, or unreported damages, enabling corrective actions like staff training or process revision. Additionally, hospitals must have clear policies for the re-issue, condemnation, and disposal of worn-out linen. Linen that is still usable after proper laundering can be reissued, while damaged or excessively worn items are condemned following standardized procedures and disposed of in an environmentally safe and hygienic manner. Such structured linen management not only improves infection control and patient satisfaction but also supports cost control and efficient inventory planning in healthcare settings.

Quality Control and Safety Measures

Ensuring quality control and safety in hospital linen management is critical to maintaining high standards of hygiene and preventing hospital-acquired infections. Hospitals must strictly adhere to established accreditation standards such as NABH (National Accreditation Board for Hospitals & Healthcare Providers), JCI (Joint Commission International), or relevant national health guidelines. These standards provide comprehensive frameworks that dictate best practices for laundering, handling, and managing hospital linen to ensure patient safety and regulatory compliance.

One important method to verify the effectiveness of disinfection processes is the use of biological indicators, which test sterilization cycles by detecting the presence or absence of microbial spores after treatment. Additionally, hospitals conduct routine microbial swab testing on cleaned linen, which involves collecting samples from laundered fabrics to assess bacterial contamination levels, thereby ensuring that the laundry processes meet strict infection control criteria.

A key aspect of maintaining safety and quality is the periodic training of laundry staff. This training educates them on updated infection control protocols, proper handling techniques, use of personal protective equipment (PPE), and emergency procedures, thereby reducing the risk of contamination and cross-infection. Furthermore, hospitals implement color coding and tagging systems for linen tracking, which help in segregating linen based on its usage area (e.g., general wards, isolation units) and laundering status (clean vs. soiled). These systems streamline the workflow, reduce errors, and prevent mix-ups, thereby enhancing overall safety and operational efficiency in linen management.

Environmental and Sustainability Practices

In modern hospital linen management, incorporating environmental and sustainability practices is essential to minimize ecological impact while maintaining hygiene standards. One important approach is the use of eco-friendly detergents and biodegradable cleaning agents that are less harmful to aquatic life and reduce chemical pollution. These detergents are formulated to be effective at lower concentrations, thereby reducing the overall chemical load discharged into the environment. Additionally, many hospitals are adopting low-water consumption technologies, such as high-efficiency washing machines and optimized washing cycles, which significantly reduce water usage compared to traditional methods.

To further manage environmental impact, hospitals install Effluent Treatment Plants (ETPs) that treat wastewater generated from laundry operations before releasing it into municipal sewage systems or natural water bodies. ETPs help remove harmful chemicals, pathogens, and suspended solids, ensuring that discharged water meets environmental safety norms and prevents contamination of surrounding ecosystems. Alongside this, hospitals focus on the reuse and recycling of water wherever possible, such as capturing and treating greywater from laundry processes for non-potable uses like cleaning floors or landscaping, thus conserving precious freshwater resources.

Energy consumption is another major factor, and many hospitals have started adopting solar dryers and energy-efficient laundry machines to reduce their carbon footprint. Solar dryers utilize renewable solar energy to dry linens, cutting down on electricity usage, while energy-efficient machines optimize power consumption without compromising washing quality. These combined sustainability initiatives not only contribute to environmental conservation but also lead to cost savings in utility bills and promote the hospital's commitment to green healthcare practices.

Challenges in Hospital Laundry Management

Hospital laundry management faces several critical challenges that impact both operational efficiency and patient safety. One of the foremost challenges is handling infectious linen safely, which becomes especially crucial during pandemics or outbreaks of contagious diseases. Proper segregation, safe transportation, and effective disinfection protocols must be strictly followed to prevent cross-contamination and protect laundry staff from exposure to pathogens. This requires continuous training and adherence to infection control guidelines, which can be resource-intensive.

Another major challenge is cost management without compromising on quality. Hospitals must balance the need for high standards of cleanliness and hygiene with budget constraints. This includes selecting detergents, disinfectants, and equipment that are both effective and affordable, as well as optimizing resource use to avoid unnecessary expenses. At the same time, managing issues such as linen theft, damage, and wastage is critical. Linen loss can result from misplacement, theft, or excessive wear and tear, which not only increases replacement costs but also disrupts inventory levels.

High-demand departments like emergency, ICU, and surgical units require quick turnaround times for linen supply, adding pressure on laundry operations to deliver clean linens promptly without compromising quality. Ensuring timely service is challenging, particularly during peak patient loads or emergencies. Moreover, the maintenance of laundry machinery and equipment poses another significant hurdle. Regular servicing and repairs are essential to avoid breakdowns, but these must be managed cost-effectively to prevent escalating maintenance expenses while ensuring uninterrupted laundry services. Balancing all these challenges requires careful planning, robust management systems, and continuous monitoring to maintain smooth hospital laundry operations.

Integration with Hospital Administration

The hospital laundry service operates as an integral part of the overall hospital administration, requiring seamless coordination with multiple departments to ensure smooth and effective functioning. One of the key linkages is with the Infection Control Unit, which plays a critical role in training laundry staff on proper handling, disinfection protocols, and compliance with infection prevention standards. This collaboration helps minimize the risk of hospital-acquired infections by ensuring that all linen is processed in accordance with stringent hygiene norms.

The Housekeeping department is another essential partner, working closely with laundry services to monitor linen usage patterns, maintain cleanliness, and address issues related to soiled linen collection and distribution. This coordination helps optimize linen flow and maintain a clean hospital environment. Meanwhile, the Nursing staff provides valuable feedback on the quality, availability, and suitability of linens, which helps the laundry service to adjust inventory and meet patient care requirements efficiently.

On the technical front, the Biomedical and Maintenance departments are responsible for the regular upkeep, repair, and servicing of laundry machinery and equipment, ensuring that operations remain uninterrupted and machines function optimally. Without their support, machinery breakdowns could lead to delays and compromised service quality. Furthermore, the laundry service depends heavily on the Procurement department for timely acquisition of quality linens, detergents, and chemicals, as well as for managing vendor contracts and ensuring cost-effective supply chains. Effective integration across these departments fosters a collaborative environment that enhances operational efficiency, cost management, and the overall quality of hospital services.

Laundry Services in hospitals, though non-clinical in nature, have a direct impact on patient care, safety, and hospital operations. The presence of clean, disinfected, and well-maintained linen enhances the healing environment, contributes to infection prevention, and promotes patient dignity. For hospital administrators, effective laundry services require careful planning, adequate infrastructure, trained manpower, and strict adherence to quality and hygiene protocols. In the modern healthcare context, hospitals must also focus on automation, sustainability, and integration with digital inventory systems to make laundry services more efficient, reliable, and eco-conscious. A high-functioning laundry department is a backbone of hospital support services and a silent yet crucial contributor to clinical excellence.

Supportive services such as the Medical Records Department, Central Sterilization and Supply Department (CSSD), Pharmacy, Food Services, and Laundry Services form the backbone of any hospital's operational efficiency and quality healthcare delivery. Though these departments function behind the scenes, their contribution is indispensable to the overall functioning of clinical services and patient outcomes.

The Medical Records Department ensures the accurate documentation, secure storage, and timely retrieval of patient information, forming the foundation for continuity of care, legal protection, research, and administration. CSSD plays a critical role in infection control by sterilizing and supplying surgical instruments, linens, and medical devices in a safe and efficient manner. A well-managed CSSD supports operating theatres, ICUs, and wards in delivering sterile care, thereby reducing hospital-acquired infections.

The Pharmacy Department is essential for procuring, storing, and dispensing medications. It ensures that patients receive the right drugs at the right time, with correct dosage and quality. Pharmacists also provide drug information and support rational use of medications, working closely with clinicians to improve therapeutic outcomes.

Food Services contribute directly to patient recovery through therapeutic nutrition, hygienic meal preparation, and personalized diet planning. The department not only supports clinical care but also enhances patient comfort and satisfaction through timely and appropriate meal service. Likewise, Laundry Services ensure a consistent supply of clean, disinfected linen for patients and staff, which is vital for hygiene, safety, and infection prevention.

Together, these departments highlight the importance of non-clinical services in a hospital setting. They complement the work of doctors and nurses by maintaining the infrastructure, hygiene, nutrition, and logistical support that make safe and efficient patient care possible. Hospital administrators must recognize, support, and continuously upgrade these services to align with modern healthcare standards, patient expectations, and accreditation requirements.

In conclusion, while these supportive services may not directly provide clinical treatment, they are essential pillars of a hospital's functionality, safety, efficiency, and overall patient experience. Their seamless integration and optimal performance are key to the success of any healthcare institution.

5. Communication and Safety Aspects in Hospital

Communication and Safety Aspects in Hospital

Communication is the lifeblood of effective hospital administration and patient care. In a complex and dynamic environment like a hospital, where various professionals interact under time-sensitive and high-stress situations, clear and structured communication becomes a necessity. Whether it's communication between doctors and patients, nurses and doctors, or administration and staff, efficient communication ensures safety, coordination, and satisfaction.

Alongside communication, safety in hospitals—particularly patient safety—is a fundamental priority. Safety protocols are closely linked to communication processes, as many medical errors occur due to poor or mismanaged communication. Hence, communication and safety are interdependent pillars of hospital administration.

Purposes of Communication in Hospitals

Communication in hospitals serves multiple purposes, ranging from clinical to administrative. The key objectives are:

1. Patient Care Coordination

- Facilitates exchange of accurate and timely information among doctors, nurses, technicians, and other staff.
- Ensures continuity and quality of care through proper documentation and handovers.

2. Enhancing Patient Experience

- Builds trust and rapport between healthcare providers and patients.
- Helps in informed decision-making through clear explanation of diagnosis, procedures, and treatment plans.

3. Operational Efficiency

- Enables smooth functioning of departments through updates, reporting, and task delegation.
- Supports scheduling, logistics, inventory, and resource management.

4. Risk Reduction and Safety

- Alerts and escalations about patient conditions, emergencies, or infections are conveyed immediately.
- Avoids clinical errors by accurate transmission of instructions and documentation.

5. Staff Coordination and Teamwork

- Promotes interdisciplinary collaboration and teamwork.
- Reduces misunderstandings, duplication of work, and conflict.

6. Legal and Ethical Compliance

- Maintains proper documentation of consent, diagnosis, treatment, and outcomes.
- Supports accountability, medico-legal defense, and accreditation requirements.

7. Training and Education

- Effective internal communication helps in regular staff training, workshops, and updates.
- Communication platforms (emails, bulletins, notice boards) are used for knowledge sharing.

Planning of Communication in Hospitals

Communication in hospitals must be **strategically planned** to ensure clarity, consistency, and reliability across departments. This involves identifying communication needs, setting goals, selecting appropriate channels, and evaluating effectiveness.

1. Communication Planning Objectives

- To standardize processes for internal and external communication.
- To reduce communication gaps that may lead to clinical errors.
- To improve efficiency in interdepartmental coordination.
- To promote transparency and responsiveness with patients and staff.

2. Elements of a Hospital Communication Plan

A. Target Audience

- Internal: Doctors, nurses, support staff, technicians, administration, maintenance teams.
- External: Patients, patient families, vendors, insurance companies, regulatory bodies.

B. Types of Communication

- Vertical Communication: Between different hierarchical levels (e.g., doctor to nurse, management to staff).
- Horizontal Communication: Between colleagues on the same level (e.g., nurse to nurse, lab to pharmacy).
- Diagonal Communication: Across different departments or functions (e.g., lab technician to nurse).

C. Communication Channels

- Verbal Communication: Face-to-face discussions, patient briefings, morning rounds, phone calls.
- Written Communication: Case notes, medical records, discharge summaries, incident reports.
- Electronic Communication: Emails, hospital information systems (HIS), telemedicine platforms.
- Visual Communication: Signboards, color codes, emergency alerts, safety posters.

D. Tools and Technologies

- Electronic Health Records (EHRs) for centralized patient data.
- Intercom systems and paging systems for quick alerts.
- Hospital Management Software (HMS) for administrative tasks.
- Mobile applications for doctor-nurse coordination and patient updates.

- CCTV and safety monitoring systems for incident documentation and security.

3. Guidelines for Effective Hospital Communication Planning

- Clarity and Brevity: Messages should be concise and understandable, especially during emergencies.
- Consistency: Information shared must be uniform across departments and staff.
- Confidentiality: Sensitive patient data must be protected under privacy laws and ethical guidelines.
- Timeliness: Information should be delivered promptly to support real-time decisions.
- Feedback Mechanisms: There should be systems to confirm that messages are received and understood.
- Language and Cultural Sensitivity: Particularly important in diverse patient populations.
- Documentation: All communication related to patient care must be recorded accurately.

4. Communication Planning for Safety and Emergency Situations

Hospitals must establish clear and effective Emergency Communication Protocols to manage critical situations promptly and efficiently, minimizing confusion and ensuring patient and staff safety. These protocols typically include standardized codes that convey specific emergencies in a concise manner. For example, Code Blue signals a cardiac arrest situation requiring immediate resuscitation efforts by the medical team. Code Red indicates a fire emergency, prompting evacuation procedures and activation of firefighting resources. Code Black alerts the hospital to a bomb threat, necessitating immediate security measures and possible evacuation. Additionally, protocols must address infection outbreaks, where rapid communication is vital to contain the spread through isolation measures and infection control strategies.

The communication during these emergencies must be swift, structured, and role-specific, ensuring that the right personnel receive the information they need without delay. Clear chains of command and designated responsibilities help reduce chaos and prevent misinformation. For instance, nurses, doctors, security, and administrative staff each have specific roles activated upon receiving these codes, which are communicated via pagers, intercoms, or dedicated emergency communication systems.

To ensure the effectiveness of these protocols, hospitals regularly conduct training programs and mock drills. These exercises familiarize staff with emergency procedures, clarify individual roles, and improve coordination among departments. Frequent drills help identify gaps or weaknesses in the communication process, allowing for continuous refinement. Ultimately, well-designed emergency communication protocols combined with rigorous training foster a culture of preparedness, enabling hospitals to respond to crises confidently and efficiently, thereby safeguarding lives and infrastructure.

5. Role of Administration in Communication Planning

The role of hospital administration in communication planning is pivotal to the smooth functioning and overall success of healthcare delivery. Hospital administrators bear the responsibility of developing and enforcing clear communication protocols that standardize how information is shared within the institution. These protocols serve as guidelines to ensure that communication is timely, accurate, and consistent across all levels—from clinical teams to administrative departments.

Administrators must also train staff in both interpersonal and digital communication skills, recognizing that effective communication goes beyond mere information exchange. Training helps healthcare workers articulate patient needs clearly, coordinate care seamlessly, and interact compassionately with patients and their families. This training also extends to the use of digital tools, such as electronic health records (EHRs), hospital intranets, and secure messaging systems, which are increasingly integral to modern hospital operations.

In addition, administrators are responsible for establishing internal communication platforms like bulletin boards, intranet portals, newsletters, and email systems that keep staff informed about hospital policies, updates, and events. These platforms help foster a culture of transparency and inclusiveness, encouraging feedback and engagement across departments.

Another critical aspect of communication planning led by administration is the creation of escalation matrices and contact hierarchies. These define who to contact in various situations and how information should flow during routine operations and emergencies. Clear escalation paths prevent confusion and delays, especially in high-pressure scenarios like critical patient care or disaster response.

Communication in hospitals transcends traditional administrative functions; it is a core element of clinical safety and service quality. Effective communication planning ensures that the right information reaches the right person at the right time, significantly reducing the risk of medical errors, which are often caused by miscommunication. It also enhances patient satisfaction by improving clarity, empathy, and responsiveness during interactions with healthcare providers.

With the increasing complexity of healthcare systems and rising patient expectations, hospitals must adopt structured and technology-enabled communication systems. Whether it involves seamless handovers between medical professionals or clear instructions for patients regarding their treatment, effective communication has a direct impact on clinical outcomes, operational efficiency, and overall safety.

For hospital administrators, prioritizing communication planning is not just a managerial task—it is an essential investment in efficiency, transparency, safety, and excellence in healthcare delivery. By fostering clear, reliable, and timely communication channels, administrators help build a resilient healthcare environment that supports high-quality patient care and promotes collaboration among multidisciplinary teams.

Modes of Communication

In hospital administration, communication plays a vital role in coordinating activities, ensuring patient safety, and enhancing the quality of healthcare services. The various modes of communication used in hospitals can be broadly categorized into verbal, non-verbal, written, and electronic forms. Verbal communication is the most immediate and widely used mode, including face-to-face conversations, telephonic discussions, and intercom systems. It is essential during patient care, team coordination, emergency situations, and clinical handovers, allowing for immediate feedback and clarification. Non-verbal communication includes body language, gestures, facial expressions, and tone of voice. It is especially important in patient interactions, where empathy, reassurance, and professionalism must be conveyed, even when words are not spoken.

Written communication is critical for accurate documentation and legal purposes. It includes medical records, prescriptions, discharge summaries, internal memos, and instructions. This mode ensures clarity, standardization, and continuity of care, especially during staff changes or follow-ups. Electronic communication has grown significantly with the advent of digital technology in healthcare. It includes emails, SMS alerts, hospital information systems (HIS), electronic medical records (EMR), and telemedicine platforms. These tools help in real-time data exchange, reduce delays in decision-making, and support remote consultations and monitoring. Hospitals also use visual communication in the form of signage, color-coded alerts, charts, and digital displays to provide directions, indicate safety instructions, or convey infection control messages.

Each of these communication modes serves specific purposes and is selected based on the context, urgency, and audience. Effective hospital communication depends on combining these modes appropriately to ensure seamless information flow, minimize errors, and promote better healthcare delivery. A strong communication system supports teamwork, improves staff efficiency, and contributes significantly to patient satisfaction and clinical outcomes.

Verbal Communication in Hospitals

Verbal communication is one of the most fundamental and frequently used forms of communication in a hospital setting. It involves the use of spoken words to convey messages, instructions, information, and emotions between healthcare professionals, patients, and administrative staff. Verbal communication in hospitals takes place in a variety of contexts such as face-to-face interactions, telephone conversations, intercom systems, morning rounds, patient consultations, emergency alerts, team briefings, and staff meetings. It is particularly vital in clinical scenarios where quick and accurate information exchange is necessary to make time-sensitive decisions that impact patient care. For instance, a surgeon is communicating with anesthetists and nurses during an operation, or a doctor discussing a treatment plan with a patient, relies heavily on verbal communication.

One of the key advantages of verbal communication is its ability to allow immediate feedback and clarification. In dynamic hospital environments, where stress and urgency are common, verbal exchanges help to resolve doubts instantly and confirm understanding, thus minimizing the risk of medical errors. It also plays a critical role in building trust and rapport with patients, where tone, empathy, and clarity of speech greatly influence patient satisfaction and cooperation. Moreover, in multidisciplinary healthcare teams, effective verbal communication ensures coordinated care, seamless shift handovers, and efficient delegation of responsibilities.

However, verbal communication can also pose challenges in a hospital context. Factors such as background noise, time constraints, language barriers, fatigue, or stress may result in misunderstandings or incomplete transmission of information. To overcome these issues, hospitals often train their staff in structured communication techniques such as SBAR (Situation, Background, Assessment, and Recommendation), which helps standardize verbal interactions, especially during critical situations. Additionally, active listening, clear articulation, appropriate tone, and use of simple, patient-friendly language are essential elements of effective verbal communication.

In conclusion, verbal communication is a cornerstone of hospital operations, directly influencing patient safety, clinical outcomes, and staff collaboration. Ensuring that healthcare workers are skilled in this mode of communication enhances teamwork, reduces errors, and promotes a culture of openness and professionalism within the hospital.

Non-Verbal Communication in Hospitals

Non-verbal communication is a powerful and indispensable part of human interaction, especially in sensitive and high-stakes environments like hospitals. It involves the transmission of messages without spoken words and includes a wide range of expressive behaviors such as facial expressions, eye contact, gestures, body posture, physical proximity, touch, tone of voice, and even professional appearance. In healthcare settings, where emotions run high and timely, compassionate care is essential, non-verbal communication plays a pivotal role in complementing, reinforcing, or even replacing verbal messages. It often serves as a bridge in situations where verbal communication is limited or ineffective, such as with patients who are unconscious, unable to speak, or have language or hearing barriers.

One of the most significant aspects of non-verbal communication in hospitals is its role in building patient trust and comfort. A caring nurse who makes gentle eye contact, maintains a calm demeanor, and uses a soft tone can immediately soothe a nervous patient far more effectively than words alone. Similarly, a physician's attentive posture, nodding, and relaxed facial expressions during a consultation can reassure the patient that they are being heard and understood. Touch is another powerful non-verbal tool—when used appropriately, a comforting hand on a patient's shoulder can convey empathy, support, and presence, especially during difficult diagnoses or emotional moments.

Among healthcare professionals, non-verbal cues play a key role in teamwork, especially during emergency procedures, surgical operations, or intensive care where communication needs to be quick and sometimes silent. Hand gestures, eye signals, or coordinated body movements are often used to indicate steps or instructions without verbal interruption. Non-verbal behavior also helps convey hierarchy, urgency, and intent. For instance, a supervisor's body language may signal authority and decisiveness, while a colleague's posture may communicate openness or collaboration. However, if non-verbal signals are inconsistent with verbal messages—for example, if a doctor tells a patient everything is fine but maintains a tense expression—this can lead to confusion or anxiety.

Cultural sensitivity is crucial in interpreting non-verbal cues correctly in hospitals. Different cultures assign different meanings to gestures, eye contact, and even physical touch. For example, while direct eye contact may be seen as confidence in some cultures, it might be perceived as disrespectful or intrusive in others. Healthcare workers must be trained to recognize and adapt to these variations to ensure respectful and effective communication across a diverse patient population.

Non-verbal communication also extends to professional appearance and hygiene, which indirectly convey a message about competence and credibility. A well-groomed healthcare worker in clean attire reflects professionalism, organization, and attention to detail—qualities patients instinctively associate with trustworthiness and capability. Furthermore, the tone and pitch of one's voice, although technically part of verbal communication, are closely related to non-verbal signals. A rushed or harsh tone can convey irritation or impatience, while a calm and soothing voice reassures patients and supports therapeutic communication.

In teaching and supervisory roles within the hospital, non-verbal communication is equally important. Educators and managers often use body language, eye contact, and gestures to maintain engagement during training sessions or staff meetings. These cues help reinforce verbal instructions and ensure clarity, especially in hands-on or skill-based training. Likewise, managers must be aware that their non-verbal behavior—such as crossed arms, frowns, or lack of eye contact—can unintentionally discourage open dialogue or create tension among staff.

In conclusion, non-verbal communication is a core competency in hospital administration and healthcare delivery. It influences the quality of patient care, the effectiveness of team coordination, and the overall atmosphere within the healthcare facility. Hospitals must invest in regular training to enhance awareness and proficiency in non-verbal communication among their staff. By doing so, they not only improve interpersonal interactions but also contribute significantly to patient satisfaction, staff morale, and the overall efficiency of the healthcare system.

Electronic Communication in Hospitals

Electronic communication has fundamentally transformed the way hospitals operate and deliver healthcare services in the 21st century. It refers to the use of digital technologies to exchange information between healthcare providers, departments, administrators, and patients. This includes a wide range of tools and systems such as emails, hospital information systems (HIS), electronic medical records (EMR), electronic health records (EHR), SMS and mobile alerts, telemedicine platforms, video conferencing, health apps, secure messaging tools, and cloud-based services. The integration of electronic communication enhances the efficiency, speed, accuracy, and accessibility of healthcare information, ultimately leading to improved patient care, better resource management, and enhanced coordination among clinical and non-clinical staff.

One of the most vital components of electronic communication in hospitals is the **Electronic Medical Record (EMR)** system. EMRs store patient-related data such as diagnosis, treatment history, laboratory results, imaging reports, prescriptions, allergies, and clinical notes in a digital format. This allows doctors, nurses, and other healthcare professionals to access a patient's medical history in real-time, from multiple locations within the hospital, thereby facilitating continuity of care and minimizing medical errors. When extended across institutions and healthcare providers, these become **Electronic Health Records (EHRs)**, supporting a more integrated healthcare ecosystem.

The **Hospital Information System (HIS)** is another crucial technology that integrates the administrative, financial, clinical, and operational aspects of hospital management. HIS enables smooth coordination among departments like outpatient and inpatient services, pharmacy, billing, diagnostics, and inventory. Automated scheduling, admission-discharge-transfer (ADT) modules, and real-time bed management improve overall hospital workflow and reduce patient waiting time. HIS ensures seamless communication between departments and helps administrators monitor key performance indicators.

Email communication is widely used for non-urgent official communication such as internal memos, policy announcements, departmental correspondence, and interdepartmental coordination. It provides a formal and traceable method of communication, which is essential in regulated environments like healthcare. Meanwhile, **SMS and mobile alerts** are used for more immediate and concise communication, such as appointment reminders, lab test availability, emergency notifications, and shift change alerts. These mobile-based alerts are especially valuable in critical care and emergency situations where time is a critical factor.

Telemedicine is another innovative application of electronic communication, allowing patients and doctors to interact remotely through video or audio conferencing. This is particularly useful in rural or underserved areas, where specialist care may not be available. Telemedicine bridges the geographical gap, enabling access to consultation, diagnosis, and follow-up care without physical travel. It is also used for post-operative monitoring, chronic disease management, and psychological counseling. During pandemics and public health emergencies, telemedicine plays a pivotal role in reducing the burden on hospitals while maintaining continuity of care.

Video conferencing tools are commonly used in hospitals for conducting virtual staff meetings, multi-disciplinary case discussions, remote training programs, and consultations with external experts. These tools help reduce travel time, allow flexible scheduling, and promote cross-institutional collaboration. **Secure instant messaging apps**, specially designed for healthcare environments, allow encrypted communication among doctors, nurses, and allied health professionals. This ensures patient confidentiality and data security in compliance with healthcare regulations such as HIPAA (in the U.S.) and NDHM (in India).

Cloud-based platforms and **healthcare portals** further extend electronic communication capabilities. Patients can log in to secure portals to view their health records, test results, make appointments, request prescriptions, or communicate with their care team. These platforms enhance patient engagement, improve adherence to treatment plans, and foster transparency in care. Additionally, **healthcare mobile apps** are being used for remote patient monitoring, medication reminders, health tracking, and lifestyle guidance.

The **use of dashboards, analytics, and automated reporting tools** enables hospital administrators to generate and analyze reports on occupancy rates, infection control, staff performance, financial indicators, and more. These data-driven insights support informed decision-making and strategic planning. Electronic communication tools also help in **clinical audits, research**, and **accreditation processes** by ensuring that documentation is systematic, complete, and easily retrievable.

Despite its numerous benefits, electronic communication in hospitals comes with certain challenges. These include system downtimes, network issues, cybersecurity threats, data breaches, and the digital divide among staff or patients unfamiliar with technology. Over-reliance on digital tools may also reduce human interaction, potentially affecting patient satisfaction. To mitigate these risks, hospitals must invest in robust IT infrastructure, provide regular training to staff, ensure data encryption and secure login protocols, and have contingency plans for system failures.

In conclusion, electronic communication is a backbone of modern hospital operations and clinical care. It enhances speed, accuracy, and coordination across departments and greatly improves the quality and safety of healthcare services. As technology continues to evolve, hospitals must embrace innovation while maintaining a balance between human touch and digital efficiency. A well-integrated electronic communication system contributes not only to administrative excellence but also to clinical effectiveness, patient satisfaction, and overall hospital performance.

Telephone communication

Telephone communication is an indispensable component of hospital administration and clinical practice, acting as one of the primary means by which information is rapidly transmitted between healthcare providers, administrative staff, patients, and external stakeholders. Its significance in a hospital setting stems from the critical need for timely, clear, and accurate communication to ensure efficient workflow, enhance patient safety, coordinate multidisciplinary care, and manage emergencies.

Within the hospital, telephones facilitate seamless internal communication across departments such as emergency, surgery, intensive care units, radiology, pharmacy, laboratory, outpatient clinics, and administration. For instance, when a patient requires urgent laboratory investigations or imaging, a nurse or doctor can instantly place a telephone call to the concerned department to prioritize the test and expedite results. Similarly, anesthetists and surgeons rely heavily on telephonic communication to coordinate surgical procedures, discuss patient status, and prepare operation theaters. This immediacy reduces delays in patient management and helps streamline hospital operations.

Modern hospitals typically use sophisticated Private Branch Exchange (PBX) systems to manage internal and external telephone communication efficiently. A PBX allows multiple phone lines and extensions to connect within the hospital, enabling staff to make interdepartmental calls without using external telephone lines. Features such as call forwarding, call conferencing, voicemail, call waiting, and speed dialing are integral to the PBX system, helping staff manage high call volumes, share information quickly, and maintain communication logs for medico-legal documentation and administrative purposes.

In addition to internal communication, telephones are vital for external communication with ambulance services, referring physicians, suppliers, regulatory authorities, and patients' families. Quick telephonic coordination with ambulance teams can significantly impact emergency response times. For example, emergency departments often communicate with paramedics en route to prepare for incoming critical patients. Likewise, hospitals communicate with insurance providers, drug suppliers, and equipment vendors to ensure uninterrupted supply of medicines and medical devices.

Telephone communication is also central to patient interaction and service delivery. Front desk staff, appointment coordinators, and call center personnel handle a large volume of calls daily for scheduling appointments, providing information about hospital services, billing queries, and follow-up instructions. Timely and courteous telephone interactions enhance patient satisfaction, reduce confusion, and improve adherence to treatment plans. Telephonic follow-up calls are routinely used to monitor patient recovery, remind patients of upcoming appointments, or provide health education.

The rise of telehealth and tele-triage services has further expanded the role of telephone communication. Healthcare professionals can assess patient symptoms remotely over the phone, guide immediate care steps, and determine the necessity of hospital visits, reducing unnecessary footfalls and minimizing infection risks. This has become especially crucial during public health crises such as the COVID-19 pandemic, where telephonic triage helps prioritize hospital resources and protect vulnerable populations.

Despite its many advantages, telephone communication in hospitals requires strict adherence to communication protocols and privacy regulations. Hospital staff must be trained to answer calls professionally, use clear and empathetic language, listen actively, and document important conversations accurately in the patient's records. Confidentiality is paramount; sensitive patient information should only be shared with authorized individuals, and conversations should be held in private areas to avoid breaches of privacy. Hospitals often implement standard operating procedures for handling telephonic communication to ensure quality, legal compliance, and patient safety.

Furthermore, challenges such as high call volumes, language barriers, technical failures, and miscommunication can impact telephone effectiveness. Therefore, continuous staff training, investment in reliable telephone infrastructure, integration with digital hospital information systems, and backup communication channels are necessary to mitigate these issues.

In conclusion, telephone communication remains a cornerstone of hospital communication systems. It enables fast, efficient, and reliable exchange of critical information that supports clinical care, administrative functions, patient engagement, and emergency response. As technology advances, telephone systems are increasingly integrated with electronic communication platforms, but their fundamental role in maintaining hospital connectivity and responsiveness continues unabated. Hospitals must prioritize maintaining and upgrading their telecommunication infrastructure and train staff rigorously to maximize the benefits of telephone communication for superior healthcare delivery.

ISDN Communication in Hospitals

Integrated Services Digital Network (ISDN) is a set of communication standards for simultaneous digital transmission of voice, video, data, and other network services over traditional telephone networks. In hospital settings, ISDN technology plays a crucial role by enabling high-quality, reliable, and versatile communication, supporting a broad range of clinical and administrative functions.

Unlike conventional analog phone lines, ISDN provides digital transmission, which results in clearer voice calls, faster connection times, and the ability to carry multiple types of data simultaneously. This is particularly beneficial in hospitals, where effective communication between departments, specialists, and external entities can impact patient outcomes and operational efficiency.

One of the primary uses of ISDN in hospitals is for telemedicine and teleconsultation services. With ISDN's capacity to transmit high-quality audio and video data, healthcare providers can conduct remote consultations, allowing specialists to assess, diagnose, and advise on patient care without the need for physical presence. This technology enables small or rural hospitals to access expertise from tertiary care centers, thereby improving access to specialized care for patients in underserved areas.

ISDN also supports video conferencing for clinical case discussions, medical education, administrative meetings, and training sessions. These video links help multidisciplinary teams collaborate efficiently, regardless of geographical distances. For example, oncologists in one city can discuss complex cases with pathologists or radiologists elsewhere, sharing imaging data and treatment plans in real time.

Beyond clinical uses, ISDN supports hospital information systems (HIS) by allowing the secure transfer of patient records, lab results, imaging files, and other electronic data between departments or with external labs and insurance companies. The simultaneous transmission of voice and data reduces delays and errors that can occur when different channels are used separately.

ISDN lines can also integrate with existing telephone systems, enhancing internal hospital communication by providing multiple digital channels over a single physical line. This allows for better call management, conferencing capabilities, and faster call setup, which is essential during emergencies or high-demand periods.

The reliability and clarity of ISDN are significant advantages in hospital settings, where communication delays or poor-quality calls can adversely affect patient care. ISDN's built-in error correction and digital encoding reduce noise and distortion, ensuring messages are accurately conveyed.

However, with the rapid rise of broadband internet and newer technologies like Voice over IP (VoIP), ISDN use is gradually declining in some regions. Yet, in many hospitals, especially those requiring dedicated and secure communication lines, ISDN remains a preferred option due to its stability, security, and quality of service.

In summary, ISDN communication in hospitals facilitates high-quality voice, video, and data transmission, supporting telemedicine, video conferencing, secure data exchange, and efficient internal communications. It bridges gaps in healthcare delivery, promotes interdisciplinary collaboration, and enhances hospital operational efficiency, ultimately contributing to improved patient care outcomes.

Public Address Communication in Hospitals

The Public Address (PA) system is a crucial mode of communication in hospital settings, designed to broadcast messages clearly and quickly to a wide audience across various hospital areas. This system uses strategically placed loudspeakers connected to a central control unit, allowing administrators or designated staff to deliver announcements, alerts, and important instructions throughout the hospital premises.

In hospitals, the PA system serves multiple critical functions. Primarily, it is used for emergency communication. In situations such as fire outbreaks, medical emergencies (e.g., Code Blue for cardiac arrest), disaster management, or evacuation drills, the PA system ensures that urgent messages reach all healthcare workers, patients, and visitors simultaneously and without delay. This instant communication helps coordinate rapid responses, mobilize emergency teams, and maintain safety protocols, which can be life-saving in time-critical scenarios.

Apart from emergencies, the PA system is employed for routine announcements such as informing about visiting hours, calling patients for appointments or diagnostic tests, shift change alerts, and public health messages. It facilitates smooth hospital operations by disseminating information to staff scattered across large buildings, wards, waiting areas, and administrative offices where direct communication may be impractical or time-consuming.

Another important use of PA systems in hospitals is to provide general information and instructions during peak periods or special events. For example, during vaccination drives or health awareness campaigns, announcements can be broadcast to guide patients, manage queues, or promote health education. This improves patient experience by keeping people informed and reducing confusion or overcrowding.

Modern PA systems in hospitals are often integrated with other communication and safety technologies. They may be linked to fire alarm systems so that automatic emergency messages play when alarms are triggered. Some systems support zoned paging, allowing announcements to be directed to specific areas only (such as an ICU or maternity ward) without disturbing other parts of the hospital. This ensures that messages are relevant and minimizes unnecessary noise in sensitive zones.

Sound quality and clarity are paramount for PA systems in hospitals. Speakers are usually installed to provide even coverage without echo or distortion, ensuring that messages are audible and intelligible, even in noisy or busy environments. Some hospitals use visual displays alongside PA announcements to aid hearing-impaired individuals.

While highly effective, PA communication requires careful management to avoid overuse or misuse, which can lead to alarm fatigue or desensitization among staff and patients. Clear protocols about who can use the system, for what types of messages, and how frequently, help maintain its effectiveness.

In conclusion, the Public Address system is an essential communication tool in hospitals. It enables quick, wide-reaching dissemination of emergency alerts, operational messages, and public information, supporting patient safety, staff coordination, and efficient hospital functioning. When designed and managed properly, PA communication significantly enhances a hospital's ability to respond to emergencies and maintain smooth day-to-day operations.

Piped Music Communication in Hospitals

Piped music is an important, though often overlooked, mode of communication within hospitals that contributes significantly to the overall environment and patient experience. Unlike direct verbal or emergency communication systems, piped music provides a continuous background audio presence that can influence mood, reduce stress, and enhance the ambiance in various hospital areas.

Hospitals are inherently stressful places, not only for patients but also for their families and the staff. Piped music systems are installed in waiting rooms, lobbies, corridors, outpatient departments, and even some patient care areas to create a calming and comforting atmosphere. Soft, soothing music such as classical, instrumental, or nature sounds is often chosen to reduce anxiety and promote relaxation. This psychological benefit can positively impact patient recovery, pain management, and overall satisfaction with care.

The therapeutic effects of music in healthcare settings are supported by research. Music therapy, supported by piped music, can lower blood pressure, decrease heart rate, and alleviate feelings of fear or depression. This is especially beneficial in pediatric wards, maternity units, and palliative care where patients and families often face heightened emotional stress.

Beyond patient well-being, piped music helps improve the working environment for hospital staff. A pleasant auditory environment can reduce fatigue and enhance concentration during long shifts, indirectly contributing to better patient care. Additionally, piped music can mask unpleasant noises typical in hospitals, such as equipment sounds, footsteps, or conversations, thereby creating a more serene and dignified environment.

From an operational perspective, piped music systems are designed to cover extensive areas through strategically placed speakers, ensuring even sound distribution without causing disturbances. The volume levels are carefully controlled to remain low enough to avoid interference with verbal communication or alarm signals but sufficient to be clearly audible.

Some hospitals also use piped music to support special occasions or cultural events, playing themed music during holidays or celebrations to foster a sense of community and uplift morale among patients and staff.

However, the choice of music must be sensitive to cultural and individual preferences. Hospitals may provide different music zones or options, or occasionally pause piped music during critical situations where silence is necessary, such as during surgical procedures or patient consultations.

In conclusion, piped music communication in hospitals plays a subtle yet vital role in enhancing the healing environment. By creating a soothing ambiance, reducing stress, and improving both patient and staff experience, piped music contributes positively to holistic healthcare delivery. When thoughtfully implemented and managed, it complements other communication systems to support a compassionate and patient-friendly hospital atmosphere.

CCTV Security in Hospitals

In modern hospital administration, ensuring the safety and security of patients, staff, visitors, and hospital property is of paramount importance. Hospitals, as complex and dynamic environments, face unique security challenges due to the sensitive nature of healthcare delivery, the presence of vulnerable patients, expensive equipment, and valuable pharmaceutical supplies. To address these concerns effectively, many hospitals rely on Closed-Circuit Television (CCTV) systems as a core component of their security infrastructure.

Purpose and Importance of CCTV in Hospitals

CCTV systems provide continuous, real-time surveillance of hospital premises, enabling security teams to monitor activity, prevent unauthorized access, and respond promptly to any incidents. This surveillance is critical for protecting various high-risk areas including emergency rooms, intensive care units (ICUs), neonatal units, pharmacies, administrative offices, parking lots, entrances, and corridors.

The presence of CCTV cameras acts as a **powerful deterrent** against theft, violence, vandalism, and other criminal activities. Hospitals frequently store expensive medical equipment and controlled drugs, making them targets for theft or tampering. CCTV helps safeguard these assets by capturing evidence and alerting security personnel to suspicious behavior.

Furthermore, hospitals often face challenges related to **crowd management**, particularly in emergency departments, outpatient areas, and during visiting hours. CCTV monitoring allows security teams to observe crowd flow and intervene if overcrowding, aggressive behavior, or unauthorized gatherings occur, ensuring a safe and orderly environment.

Applications and Benefits

1. **Real-Time Monitoring and Rapid Response**

   CCTV cameras feed live video to a central security control room staffed 24/7 by trained personnel. This real-time monitoring enables immediate identification of incidents such as unauthorized entry, patient elopement, aggressive visitors, or suspicious packages. Security staff can dispatch guards or alert hospital administration instantly, minimizing risks and managing emergencies proactively.

2. **Incident Documentation and Investigation**

   Recorded footage from CCTV cameras serves as invaluable evidence in investigating accidents, disputes, or criminal acts within the hospital. For example, if a patient claims negligence or if there is a theft in the pharmacy, video recordings can provide clear, objective information to clarify events. This evidence supports internal reviews, insurance claims, and legal proceedings, promoting accountability and transparency.

3. **Access Control and Restricted Areas**

   Certain hospital zones require restricted access for safety and privacy reasons—such as operating theaters, drug storage rooms, neonatal units, and administrative offices. CCTV systems integrated with access control technologies (like card readers and biometric scanners) monitor who enters these sensitive areas, ensuring only authorized personnel gain entry. This reduces risks of contamination, theft, and breaches of patient confidentiality.

4. **Supporting Patient Safety**

Beyond security, CCTV cameras enhance patient safety. For example, in psychiatric wards or geriatric units, cameras help staff monitor patients who may be at risk of falls, self-harm, or wandering away. Video surveillance allows quicker interventions in emergencies without constant physical supervision, balancing safety with patient dignity.

5. **Integration with Other Security Systems**

Modern CCTV systems are integrated with fire alarms, emergency communication networks, and building management systems. When a fire alarm triggers, the CCTV system can automatically focus cameras on evacuation routes or affected areas to assist fire response teams. Similarly, integration with Public Address systems allows security staff to make real-time announcements in response to incidents.

Technology and Features

Hospitals utilize a range of advanced CCTV technologies designed specifically to address the complex security and monitoring needs of healthcare environments. One of the key features is high-resolution cameras, which capture clear and detailed images essential for accurately identifying individuals, monitoring activities, and investigating incidents. The clarity provided by these cameras is especially important in critical areas such as emergency rooms, pharmacies, and entrances where security breaches or suspicious activities must be quickly recognized and addressed.

To ensure round-the-clock surveillance, hospitals also employ infrared and night vision cameras. These specialized cameras allow continuous monitoring even in low-light or completely dark conditions, such as parking lots during night shifts or less frequented corridors. This capability is vital to maintain safety and security at all hours, protecting both patients and staff.

Another sophisticated technology is the Pan-Tilt-Zoom (PTZ) cameras, which offer operators the flexibility to remotely control camera movements—panning horizontally, tilting vertically, and zooming in on areas or individuals of interest. This dynamic control allows security personnel to track moving targets or focus on suspicious behavior without needing multiple fixed cameras, making surveillance more efficient and comprehensive.

Modern CCTV systems also integrate motion detection and intelligent analytics software that can automatically detect unusual activities or movements in designated zones. For example, if someone enters a restricted area, the system immediately sends alerts to security staff, enabling rapid intervention before any security breach escalates. These smart features reduce the need for constant manual monitoring and help prioritize attention to critical events.

With the advancement of network technologies, remote monitoring has become a standard feature in hospital CCTV systems. Authorized personnel can securely access live video feeds or recorded footage anytime and from anywhere via encrypted mobile apps or web portals. This flexibility is invaluable during emergencies or off-hours when on-site security might be limited, ensuring that surveillance is never compromised.

Finally, secure data storage and backup solutions are integral to hospital CCTV operations. Recorded footage is stored safely with encryption to protect against tampering or unauthorized access. Hospitals maintain these recordings according to their internal policies and legal regulations, often retaining footage for a specified duration to support investigations, audits, or compliance reviews. Robust storage management also ensures that data is retrievable when needed while optimizing storage space and costs.

Together, these technologies form a comprehensive, reliable security system that supports hospital safety, protects patients and staff, and helps administrators manage risk proactively and efficiently.

Privacy and Ethical Considerations

While CCTV systems play a critical role in enhancing security within hospital environments, it is equally important to uphold the privacy and dignity of patients, visitors, and staff. Hospitals face the ethical challenge of balancing the need for surveillance with respect for individual rights and confidentiality. To address this, strict guidelines and protocols must be followed to ensure that CCTV usage does not infringe upon personal privacy or lead to misuse of sensitive information.

One of the foremost considerations is the careful avoidance of installing cameras in private patient areas. These spaces include patient wards, bathrooms, changing rooms, and any other locations where individuals expect a high degree of privacy. Installing cameras in such areas would be a serious breach of ethical standards and could expose hospitals to legal liabilities. Surveillance should be strictly limited to public and semi-public spaces, such as hospital corridors, lobbies, entrances, waiting areas, and parking lots, where security monitoring is necessary and less intrusive.

Transparency is another crucial aspect. Hospitals must inform patients, visitors, and staff about the presence and purpose of CCTV systems through clear signage and communication policies. This openness helps build trust and ensures that individuals are aware their movements may be recorded for safety reasons, thereby reducing concerns or misunderstandings related to covert surveillance.

Access to CCTV footage must be strictly controlled and limited to authorized personnel who have legitimate reasons to review the recordings, such as security officers or hospital administrators. Ensuring this restricted access protects against unauthorized viewing or misuse of data. Furthermore, hospitals must comply with applicable data protection regulations, such as HIPAA in the United States, which governs the privacy of health information, or the GDPR in Europe, which sets strict rules on personal data handling. These laws mandate rigorous safeguards around the collection, storage, and sharing of video footage, especially when it may include identifiable patient information.

Hospitals also need to establish clear policies on the retention, use, and disposal of CCTV footage. Footage should only be kept for a legally justified period, after which it must be securely deleted or destroyed to prevent unnecessary accumulation of personal data. The intended use of recordings should be well-defined—for example, footage may be retained for security investigations but not used for unrelated purposes such as employee surveillance without consent.

By integrating these privacy and ethical considerations into their CCTV strategies, hospitals can ensure that security measures protect not only physical safety but also the rights and dignity of everyone within the healthcare environment. This balanced approach helps maintain a trusting and respectful atmosphere essential for quality patient care and institutional integrity.

Challenges and Best Practices

Hospitals face multiple challenges in implementing and managing effective CCTV systems, each requiring careful attention to ensure security objectives are met without compromising operational efficiency or trust. One significant challenge is the volume of data generated. Large healthcare facilities operate numerous cameras 24/7, producing massive amounts of video footage daily. Managing this data demands robust storage infrastructure capable of handling high-capacity, high-speed recording. Additionally, efficient retrieval systems are essential so that relevant footage can be accessed quickly during investigations or audits without overwhelming IT resources. Hospitals must therefore invest in scalable digital video recorders (DVRs) or network video recorders (NVRs), often supplemented with cloud storage solutions, while balancing cost and data privacy requirements.

Another key challenge is staff training. It is not enough to install advanced CCTV technology; hospital security personnel and relevant staff must be adequately trained to monitor live feeds, interpret video data accurately, and respond swiftly and appropriately to suspicious activities or emergencies. Misinterpretation of footage or delayed responses can compromise safety and negate the benefits of surveillance. Training programs should also cover ethical considerations, patient privacy laws, and proper use of equipment to ensure compliance and professionalism in monitoring activities.

Technical maintenance presents an ongoing operational hurdle. CCTV systems require regular inspections to check camera functionality, clean lenses, recalibrate angles, and update software. Maintenance must address potential blind spots, lighting issues, and equipment wear-and-tear before these gaps create security vulnerabilities. Prompt troubleshooting and repair protocols are vital to minimize downtime. Hospitals must also prepare for equipment upgrades to keep pace with evolving technology and emerging security threats, which requires budgeting and coordination with vendors.

Finally, hospitals must be mindful of avoiding over-surveillance. While surveillance is essential for safety, excessive monitoring can lead to staff discomfort, decreased morale, and erosion of patient trust. Intrusive or continuous surveillance might be perceived as a lack of confidence in employees, creating a stressful work environment. Patients and visitors may also feel their privacy is compromised if cameras are placed inappropriately or if surveillance is too pervasive. Striking a balanced approach means clearly defining surveillance zones, focusing on critical and vulnerable areas, and ensuring transparency about surveillance policies. Regular feedback from staff and patients can help administrators adjust CCTV practices to maintain security without undermining the hospital's caring environment.

In summary, addressing these challenges requires a combination of advanced technology, skilled personnel, proactive maintenance, and ethical oversight. Adopting best practices such as scalable data management, continuous staff training, scheduled maintenance programs, and a balanced surveillance policy enables hospitals to leverage CCTV effectively, ensuring safety and security while fostering trust and operational harmony.

To address these, hospitals often establish a dedicated security management team responsible for CCTV operations, policy enforcement, and continuous improvement of security protocols.

CCTV security systems are integral to the modern hospital security framework, significantly contributing to protecting lives, property, and sensitive information. By enabling constant surveillance, rapid incident response, evidence gathering, and controlled access to restricted areas, CCTV enhances hospital safety and operational efficiency. When implemented thoughtfully with attention to privacy, ethics, and technical excellence, CCTV systems help create a secure, safe, and welcoming healthcare environment for patients, visitors, and staff alike.

Loss Prevention in Communication Aspects in Hospitals

Effective communication is the backbone of efficient hospital administration and quality patient care. However, communication breakdowns can lead to significant losses—ranging from medical errors, financial costs, compromised patient safety, to damaged reputation. Therefore, **loss prevention in communication** refers to the strategies and measures hospitals employ to minimize errors, misunderstandings, delays, and data loss in all forms of communication within the healthcare setting.

Types of Communication Losses in Hospitals

1. **Information Loss or Miscommunication:**

   Vital patient information may be incorrectly conveyed or lost between departments or staff shifts, leading to errors in diagnosis, treatment, or medication administration.

2. **Delayed Communication:**

   Slow transfer of information can cause treatment delays, extended hospital stays, or missed critical interventions.

3. **Data Loss:**

   Loss or corruption of electronic medical records or test results due to technical failures, poor data handling, or inadequate backup systems can severely impact patient care.

4. **Confidentiality Breaches:**

   Improper handling or communication of sensitive patient data can lead to privacy violations and legal penalties.

5. **Misinterpretation:**

   Ambiguous or unclear communication, whether verbal or written, can result in errors and misunderstandings among healthcare teams.

Strategies for Loss Prevention in Communication

1. **Standardized Communication Protocols:**

   Hospitals implement structured communication tools like SBAR (Situation, Background, Assessment, Recommendation) to ensure critical information is conveyed clearly and consistently during handoffs, shift changes, or emergencies.

2. **Use of Electronic Health Records (EHRs):**

   Digitizing patient records reduces errors from illegible handwriting, misplaced files, or incomplete documentation. EHRs ensure real-time access and secure sharing of patient data across departments.

3. **Training and Education:**

   Regular staff training on effective communication skills, use of communication technologies, and confidentiality policies reduces human errors and improves clarity.

4. **Effective Use of Technology:**

   Telephone systems, intercoms, paging, email alerts, and secure messaging apps help deliver timely and accurate information. Redundant communication channels can prevent message loss.

5. **Audit and Feedback Systems:**

   Regular monitoring and evaluation of communication processes help identify gaps or recurrent errors. Feedback loops allow corrective measures and continuous improvement.

6. **Clear Documentation Practices:**

   Encouraging precise, complete, and legible documentation in patient charts, medication orders, and reports helps avoid ambiguity.

7. **Privacy and Security Measures:**

   Encrypting electronic communications, restricting data access to authorized personnel, and ensuring compliance with regulations like HIPAA protect against confidentiality breaches.

8. **Crisis Communication Plans:**

   Hospitals prepare specific communication protocols for emergencies to prevent chaos and information overload, ensuring critical messages reach all relevant staff efficiently.

Benefits of Effective Loss Prevention in Communication

- **Enhanced Patient Safety:** Reduced medical errors and adverse events due to accurate and timely information exchange.
- **Operational Efficiency:** Faster decision-making and streamlined workflows improve overall hospital performance.
- **Financial Savings:** Minimizing errors and delays reduces unnecessary treatments, legal claims, and resource wastage.
- **Improved Staff Morale:** Clear communication reduces frustration and conflict among healthcare workers.
- **Compliance and Reputation:** Maintaining confidentiality and accurate records ensures regulatory compliance and builds public trust.

Loss prevention in hospital communication is vital for safeguarding patient health, improving care quality, and optimizing hospital operations. By adopting standardized protocols, leveraging technology, emphasizing training, and enforcing security policies, hospitals can significantly reduce the risks associated with communication failures. Effective communication loss prevention not only protects patients and staff but also strengthens the institution's credibility and sustainability in a demanding healthcare environment.

Fire Safety in Hospitals

Hospitals are highly sensitive environments where the safety of patients, staff, visitors, and expensive equipment is paramount. Fire safety in hospitals is critically important due to the presence of vulnerable patients, complex medical equipment, flammable materials, and multiple electrical devices. A fire in a hospital can have devastating consequences, including loss of life, injury, and damage to critical infrastructure. Therefore, comprehensive fire safety planning, prevention, and response measures are essential components of hospital administration.

Why Fire Safety is Crucial in Hospitals

Hospitals face several significant challenges when operating effective CCTV systems, despite their vital role in ensuring safety and security. One major issue is the sheer volume of data generated by multiple high-resolution cameras operating around the clock. Managing this vast amount of video footage requires advanced and scalable storage solutions, along with efficient indexing systems to enable quick retrieval of specific recordings during investigations or audits. Without proper management, accessing relevant footage can become time-consuming and cumbersome, potentially delaying critical responses. Another challenge lies in the training of staff responsible for monitoring and handling CCTV systems. Security personnel and hospital staff must not only be skilled in operating the equipment but also adept at interpreting footage accurately to distinguish normal activities from suspicious behavior. Comprehensive training is essential to ensure that the staff respond appropriately to incidents, handle sensitive information with confidentiality, and comply with legal and ethical standards.

Technical maintenance presents yet another hurdle, as cameras and recording devices require regular upkeep to function optimally. Environmental factors such as dust, moisture, and temperature fluctuations can impair camera performance, while blind spots in coverage can create security vulnerabilities. Routine inspections, cleaning, firmware updates, and timely repairs are necessary to avoid equipment failure and maintain continuous surveillance. Budgeting for ongoing maintenance and upgrades is therefore crucial for system reliability. Equally important is the challenge of avoiding over-surveillance, which can negatively impact staff morale and patient trust. Excessive monitoring, especially in areas close to patient care, might lead to feelings of invasion of privacy or mistrust. Hospitals must carefully balance the need for security with respect for privacy by limiting cameras to public and semi-public areas and clearly communicating surveillance policies to patients, visitors, and staff. Transparency, along with feedback mechanisms, helps maintain a respectful and secure environment.

To address these challenges, hospitals should adopt best practices such as investing in secure and compliant data storage, providing regular and updated training programs, implementing thorough maintenance schedules, and establishing clear, ethical surveillance policies. Incorporating advanced technologies like AI-driven video analytics can also enhance monitoring efficiency by flagging unusual activities automatically. By managing these aspects well, hospitals can leverage CCTV systems to improve safety without compromising ethical standards, operational efficiency, or the trust of their community.

Key Components of Fire Safety in Hospitals

1. **Fire Prevention**

   Fire prevention is the cornerstone of hospital fire safety and serves as the first and most crucial step in protecting patients, staff, and property from fire hazards. Hospitals, being complex environments with numerous electrical devices, flammable materials, and vulnerable occupants, must adopt a proactive approach to minimize the risk of fire outbreaks.

   One of the key elements of fire prevention is regular maintenance of all electrical systems and equipment. Hospitals rely heavily on medical devices, lighting, HVAC systems, and other electrical appliances that, if faulty or poorly maintained, can become significant fire hazards. Routine inspections and timely repairs of wiring, plugs, circuit breakers, and machines reduce the chances of electrical short circuits, overheating, or sparks that might ignite a fire.

   Another critical aspect is the proper storage of flammable materials. Hospitals often use oxygen cylinders, cleaning chemicals, and various medical gases and liquids that are highly combustible. These materials must be stored securely in well-ventilated, designated storage rooms that are clearly marked and have restricted access to authorized personnel only. Proper segregation of incompatible chemicals and the use of fire-resistant storage cabinets further reduce the risk of accidental ignition.

Strict enforcement of a no-smoking policy throughout the hospital premises is essential to prevent fire risks associated with careless smoking. Smoking areas, if any, must be clearly demarcated away from patient areas, oxygen storage, and other flammable zones, with adequate signage and regular monitoring to ensure compliance. Given the vulnerability of hospital patients, especially those on oxygen therapy, strict control of smoking is indispensable.

Maintaining high standards of housekeeping is equally important in fire prevention. Hospital corridors, staircases, fire exits, and emergency access routes must be kept clear of any obstructions such as equipment, furniture, or combustible waste like paper, cloth, or packaging materials. Accumulated clutter not only increases fire fuel but can also block escape routes, hampering evacuation during emergencies. Regular cleaning schedules and audits help ensure that fire exits remain accessible at all times.

Together, these fire prevention measures create a safer hospital environment by addressing potential fire risks before they escalate. Prevention minimizes the likelihood of fire incidents, protecting patients' lives, safeguarding critical healthcare infrastructure, and ensuring uninterrupted delivery of medical services. Hospital administrators must emphasize fire prevention through clear policies, ongoing staff training, and strict monitoring to build a culture of safety and vigilance.

2. **Fire Detection and Alarm Systems**

Fire detection and alarm systems are fundamental components of hospital fire safety, designed to identify the presence of fire or smoke at the earliest possible stage and promptly alert hospital personnel and occupants. Early detection is critical in healthcare settings because it allows for rapid intervention, evacuation, and firefighting, minimizing risks to vulnerable patients and valuable medical equipment.

One of the primary devices used in fire detection are smoke detectors, which are strategically installed in patient rooms, corridors, waiting areas, and other critical parts of the hospital. These detectors sense the presence of smoke particles in the air, often one of the earliest indicators of a fire, even before visible flames or significant heat develops. Because hospitals house patients who may not be able to evacuate quickly, early smoke detection is essential to trigger timely alerts and responses.

Alongside smoke detectors, heat detectors serve as an important complementary safety measure. These sensors respond to a rapid rise in temperature or when the ambient temperature crosses a preset threshold, activating the fire alarm system. Heat detectors are particularly useful in areas where smoke detectors may generate false alarms due to dust, steam, or other benign particulates, such as kitchens, laundry rooms, or boiler areas.

To empower hospital staff with direct control over fire alerting, manual call points (also called manual pull stations) are installed throughout the facility, typically near exits and in corridors. These allow any staff member who notices a fire or smoke to immediately raise the alarm by pressing a button or pulling a lever. This manual activation ensures that even if automatic detectors fail or a fire is detected visually, the hospital community can respond quickly.

All these detection devices are integrated into a centralized alarm system that consolidates signals from smoke and heat detectors, as well as manual call points. Upon activation, this system sounds audible alarms and flashes visual warning lights throughout the hospital, ensuring that staff, patients, and visitors are promptly alerted. Additionally, the centralized system often connects with the hospital's emergency response protocols by notifying security personnel, fire wardens, and local fire services automatically. It may also trigger secondary actions such as unlocking emergency exits, shutting down HVAC systems to prevent smoke spread, and activating fire suppression equipment.

Together, these fire detection and alarm components form an early warning network crucial for protecting lives, minimizing property damage, and maintaining hospital functionality during fire emergencies. Their proper installation, regular testing, and staff training on alarm procedures are vital for an effective fire safety strategy.

3. **Fire Suppression Systems**

Fire suppression systems are a critical element of hospital fire safety, designed to quickly detect, control, and extinguish fires before they can spread and cause significant damage or endanger lives. Due to the sensitive nature of hospital environments—where patients, complex medical equipment, and flammable materials coexist—these systems must be reliable, effective, and tailored to specific risks found in different areas of the facility.

One of the most common and essential fire suppression systems in hospitals is the automatic sprinkler system. These systems are equipped with sprinkler heads installed throughout the building, which automatically activate when they detect heat or smoke indicative of a fire. The sprinklers release water to suppress or extinguish the fire at its initial stages, significantly reducing fire damage and providing crucial time for safe evacuation. Their automatic nature means they can respond even if the fire occurs when no personnel are immediately present, offering continuous protection.

In addition to sprinklers, hospitals are equipped with fire extinguishers, which are portable and strategically placed in accessible locations throughout the facility. Different types of extinguishers—such as water-based, carbon dioxide (CO_2), and dry powder—are selected based on the specific fire risks of an area. For instance, water extinguishers are suitable for ordinary combustibles like paper or cloth, CO_2 extinguishers are effective for electrical fires, and dry powder extinguishers are versatile and can handle flammable liquids and gases. Staff are trained in their proper use to ensure quick and effective response to small fires.

Fire hose reels are another vital component, installed in various parts of the hospital for use by trained personnel or fire services. These hoses provide a steady stream of water to tackle fires that may require more sustained efforts than portable extinguishers can provide. Their accessibility and ease of use make them an important resource for initial firefighting until professional firefighters arrive.

Moreover, hospitals often install specialized fire suppression systems in sensitive areas such as data centers, operating rooms, or areas housing critical electronic equipment. These systems might use gas-based suppression agents like FM-200, inert gases, or clean agents that extinguish fires without water, which could otherwise damage delicate medical instruments and electronics. Such systems are carefully designed to quickly suppress fires while minimizing harm to equipment and personnel.

Overall, the integration of multiple fire suppression systems—automatic sprinklers, extinguishers, hose reels, and specialized technologies—forms a comprehensive fire safety network. This layered approach ensures rapid detection, immediate containment, and effective control of fires, protecting lives, safeguarding valuable equipment, and maintaining hospital operations during emergencies.

4. **Evacuation Procedures and Fire Drills**

Evacuation procedures and fire drills are vital components of hospital fire safety, designed to ensure that in the event of a fire emergency, patients, staff, and visitors can be moved to safety efficiently and without confusion. Given the complexity of hospital environments—where immobile patients, sensitive equipment, and large numbers of people coexist—evacuation plans must be meticulously tailored to the specific building layout and the unique needs of its occupants.

A critical element of these procedures is the establishment of clearly marked and unobstructed evacuation routes. These pathways and emergency exits must be visible, easily accessible, and free from any obstacles at all times. Signage should be strategically placed to guide everyone—even those unfamiliar with the building—toward the safest and quickest exit points. The routes must also consider patient mobility; for example, corridors wide enough for wheelchairs and stretchers, as well as ramps instead of stairs where possible.

Hospitals also designate specific assembly points—safe, open areas away from the building—where all evacuees gather after leaving the premises. These assembly points serve multiple purposes: they allow for an accurate headcount to ensure everyone has evacuated safely, provide a location for emergency responders to organize, and facilitate communication among hospital personnel and emergency teams.

Another essential aspect of evacuation planning is the appointment and training of fire wardens. These trained staff members have the responsibility to coordinate the evacuation process within their designated zones. They assist patients, particularly those who are immobile or critically ill, by guiding them along evacuation routes, calming them to prevent panic, and helping maintain order during the evacuation. Fire wardens also perform a critical role in ensuring that all personnel and patients are accounted for once outside the building.

Regularly conducted fire drills are indispensable in reinforcing the evacuation plan. These drills simulate real emergency conditions and train staff on their specific roles, such as operating firefighting equipment, assisting patients, and guiding others along escape routes. They help familiarize everyone with the procedures, identify any weaknesses or bottlenecks in the plan, and improve response times. Additionally, fire drills foster a culture of preparedness and vigilance, reducing panic and confusion if a real fire occurs.

In summary, well-planned evacuation procedures supported by regular fire drills are crucial for minimizing risks, protecting lives, and ensuring that a hospital can respond swiftly and effectively during fire emergencies.

5. **Training and Awareness**

Training and awareness play a crucial role in ensuring effective fire safety within hospitals, where the stakes are especially high due to the presence of vulnerable patients and complex infrastructure. It is essential that all hospital staff, including medical, administrative, housekeeping, and security personnel, are thoroughly educated and regularly trained on fire safety protocols to prevent fire incidents and respond appropriately if they occur.

Firstly, staff must be trained to recognize potential fire hazards commonly found in hospital settings, such as overloaded electrical outlets, improper storage of flammable materials, malfunctioning equipment, and blocked fire exits. Understanding these risks enables employees to take proactive measures to eliminate or mitigate hazards before they escalate into emergencies.

Additionally, comprehensive training on the use of fire safety equipment is vital. This includes hands-on instruction on how to operate different types of fire extinguishers correctly, activate fire alarms, and use emergency communication systems. Staff who are confident in using these tools can act quickly to contain small fires or alert others, potentially preventing major disasters.

A critical component of fire safety training is preparing staff to assist patients during evacuations. This requires special emphasis on safely moving immobile, critically ill, or differently-abled patients, ensuring their safety without causing panic or injury. Training programs often include role-playing or simulation exercises where staff practice patient evacuation routes, use of evacuation chairs, and coordination with emergency responders.

Moreover, staff must be aware of the importance of promptly reporting any fire hazards, smoke, or fire incidents. Early detection and communication can make a significant difference in preventing the spread of fire and ensuring timely emergency response. Clear guidelines should be provided on whom to notify and the steps to take during such events.

Regular refresher courses and mock drills are essential to maintain a high level of preparedness and reinforce knowledge among hospital employees. These exercises help identify gaps in understanding or response protocols and foster a culture of safety and vigilance. Overall, continuous training and awareness empower hospital staff to act decisively, protect lives, and minimize damage during fire emergencies, making it an indispensable part of hospital safety management.

6. **Coordination with Fire Services**

Coordination with fire services is a vital component of hospital fire safety planning, ensuring that emergency response is swift, effective, and well-informed. Hospitals actively establish strong liaisons and communication channels with their local fire departments to facilitate a seamless partnership in the event of a fire or related emergency. This collaboration allows firefighters to become familiar with the hospital's unique environment before an emergency occurs, which is critical given the complexity and sensitivity of healthcare facilities.

A key aspect of this coordination is providing fire services with detailed and up-to-date hospital layouts, including floor plans, locations of critical departments such as intensive care units, operating theaters, hazardous material storage, and areas with vulnerable or immobile patients. Having this information readily available enables firefighters to plan and execute rescue operations efficiently, minimizing delays and potential confusion during high-pressure situations. Hospitals often conduct joint drills and simulations with fire personnel, which help familiarize the responders with entry points, stairwells, fire exits, and any architectural peculiarities that might impact firefighting efforts.

Moreover, hospitals inform fire departments about the presence and locations of any hazardous materials, such as flammable gases, chemicals, or biomedical waste, which require special handling and precautions. This knowledge helps firefighters tailor their approach to safely control and contain fires without causing additional risks to patients, staff, or the environment. In some cases, hospitals may also coordinate access to backup power systems, elevators, and ventilation controls with fire services to support firefighting and evacuation activities.

In addition to providing information, continuous communication channels are maintained to ensure quick alerts and updates during an emergency. Hospitals may assign specific staff members as points of contact for the fire department, streamlining coordination and decision-making. This relationship is also essential for post-incident reviews, allowing both parties to analyze the response, identify areas for improvement, and update protocols accordingly.

Ultimately, the collaboration between hospitals and fire services is a proactive measure that significantly enhances fire safety preparedness. By ensuring that firefighters are well-informed and integrated into hospital emergency plans, this coordination helps save lives, protect critical infrastructure, and reduce the overall impact of fire incidents on healthcare delivery.

Hospitals establish liaisons with local fire departments to ensure rapid response during emergencies. Firefighters should have access to hospital layouts, hazardous areas, and patient locations.

Challenges in Hospital Fire Safety

Challenges in hospital fire safety are complex and multifaceted, largely due to the unique environment and vulnerable population that hospitals serve. One of the most critical challenges is the safe and rapid evacuation of immobile or critically ill patients. Unlike other buildings, hospitals house patients who may be bedridden, connected to life-support machines, or otherwise unable to move independently. Evacuating these patients requires specialized equipment, well-trained staff, and meticulously planned protocols to prevent panic and ensure patient safety. This task becomes even more difficult during a fire emergency when time is of the essence and conditions such as smoke, heat, and reduced visibility pose additional hazards.

Another significant challenge is the need to maintain fire safety systems without disrupting sensitive medical equipment. Many hospitals rely on advanced machines such as ventilators, dialysis units, and imaging devices that are sensitive to environmental changes or electrical interruptions. Fire safety measures like sprinkler systems, alarms, and smoke detectors must be designed and installed carefully to avoid damage to such equipment or unintended interference with their operation, which could jeopardize patient care.

Maintaining fire safety protocols during peak hours or other emergencies also presents considerable difficulties. Hospitals often operate 24/7 with high patient turnover, visiting hours, and staff shifts. During busy times, the movement of people—patients, visitors, and staff—can complicate evacuation plans and hinder the swift implementation of safety procedures. Furthermore, in situations where other emergencies occur simultaneously (e.g., a power outage or medical emergency), coordinating fire safety measures becomes even more challenging.

Architectural constraints pose another major obstacle in hospital fire safety. Hospitals are typically large, multi-story complexes with basements, restricted access zones, and specialized areas like operating theaters and intensive care units. Navigating these spaces during a fire requires detailed knowledge of the layout and clear signage. Restricted zones may limit rescue access, while multiple floors and basements can slow evacuation efforts and complicate the deployment of firefighting resources. Retrofitting older hospital buildings to meet modern fire safety standards is often costly and logistically difficult, further exacerbating these challenges.

Overall, ensuring effective fire safety in hospitals demands a comprehensive, multidisciplinary approach. It requires continuous staff training, rigorous maintenance of fire safety equipment, clear emergency communication, and architectural designs that facilitate rapid evacuation without compromising patient care or equipment functionality. Only through proactive planning and coordination can hospitals overcome these challenges and protect their vulnerable populations from the devastating consequences of fire incidents.

Fire safety in hospitals is an indispensable aspect of healthcare facility management, directly impacting patient safety, staff well-being, and infrastructure protection. It requires a comprehensive approach combining fire prevention, early detection, effective suppression, well-planned evacuation, ongoing staff training, and coordination with emergency services. By prioritizing fire safety and continuously updating protocols, hospitals can minimize the risks and consequences of fire incidents, ensuring a safer environment for all occupants.

Alarm Systems in Hospitals

Alarm systems play a critical role in hospital safety management by providing timely alerts to staff, patients, and visitors about emergencies or abnormal conditions. These systems are designed to detect and communicate incidents such as fires, unauthorized access, equipment failures, patient emergencies, and environmental hazards. An effective alarm system enhances hospital preparedness, speeds up response times, and helps safeguard lives and property.

Purpose of Alarm Systems in Hospitals

1. Early Detection and Notification of Fire and Smoke

One of the most vital purposes of alarm systems in hospitals is the early detection of fire and smoke, which can pose catastrophic risks. Hospitals house a vulnerable population including critically ill patients, newborns, elderly persons, and individuals with mobility impairments, making fire safety paramount. Smoke or fire alarms serve to detect the earliest signs of a fire — such as the presence of smoke particles or elevated temperatures — before the situation escalates.

Importance of Early Warning

Early detection allows hospital staff to initiate immediate evacuation protocols, activate fire suppression systems, and notify emergency services without delay. This minimizes potential casualties and damage to critical infrastructure. The alarm system is designed to trigger audible alerts, flashing lights, and sometimes verbal instructions throughout the hospital to ensure that all occupants, including those who may be sleeping or in sound-isolated areas, become aware of the danger promptly.

Integration with Fire Safety Protocols

Alarm systems integrate with other fire safety measures, such as automatic sprinkler activation, smoke control systems, and emergency lighting. This integrated approach ensures a comprehensive response aimed at containment, evacuation, and rescue, significantly improving survival rates and property protection.

2. Signaling Medical Emergencies

Hospitals are settings where urgent medical situations requiring immediate intervention occur frequently. Alarm systems are indispensable in alerting medical personnel about critical patient conditions that demand rapid response.

Code Alerts and Medical Emergency Signals

Hospitals employ standardized codes (e.g., Code Blue for cardiac arrest, Code Red for fire) transmitted through alarm systems to convey specific emergency types. These codes facilitate quick identification of the emergency type without causing panic among patients and visitors.

For instance, a **Code Blue alarm** alerts trained resuscitation teams to a patient experiencing cardiac arrest or respiratory failure, enabling immediate mobilization of equipment and personnel to the patient's bedside. This rapid response is critical in improving patient survival chances during life-threatening conditions.

Enhancing Patient Safety and Outcomes

Alarm systems linked to patient monitoring devices continuously track vital signs such as heart rate, oxygen saturation, and blood pressure. When these parameters fall outside safe ranges, alarms sound to alert nurses and doctors to intervene before the patient's condition worsens. This proactive alert system enhances patient safety by reducing the likelihood of unnoticed deterioration.

3. Notifying Security Breaches and Unauthorized Entries

Hospitals are also tasked with maintaining secure environments for patients, staff, and sensitive information. Alarm systems contribute to hospital security by detecting unauthorized access and potential security threats.

Perimeter and Access Control Alarms

Security alarms are installed at entry points, restricted zones (e.g., pharmacies, operating theaters), and sensitive areas (e.g., neonatal ICUs). These alarms activate when unauthorized persons attempt to enter or tamper with security barriers, immediately notifying security personnel to investigate and respond.

Protection of Patients and Assets

Hospitals often handle controlled substances and expensive medical equipment. Alarm systems help safeguard these assets from theft or misuse by ensuring that any security breach triggers an alert for swift action.

Incident Management and Response

Security alarms may be integrated with CCTV and access control systems, enabling real-time monitoring and rapid deployment of security teams. This integration is crucial for protecting vulnerable patients, especially in psychiatric or pediatric wards, and preventing violence or abuse.

4. Warning of Equipment Malfunctions and Environmental Dangers

Hospitals rely heavily on sophisticated medical and facility equipment that must function continuously without fail. Alarm systems are instrumental in identifying equipment malfunctions and environmental hazards that could compromise patient care or safety.

Equipment Monitoring Alarms

Medical devices such as ventilators, infusion pumps, dialysis machines, and sterilizers are equipped with built-in alarms to alert staff to operational faults, disconnections, or abnormal parameters. These alarms help prevent adverse events by prompting timely troubleshooting or replacement of malfunctioning equipment.

Environmental Hazard Detection

Hospitals also face risks from environmental hazards such as gas leaks (oxygen, anesthetic gases), chemical spills, or water leaks. Specialized sensors integrated with alarm systems can detect hazardous gas concentrations or moisture presence and activate alerts to prevent poisoning, fires, or structural damage.

Power Supply and Backup Alerts

Hospitals depend on continuous power supply for critical care areas. Alarm systems monitor electrical infrastructure, signaling power failures, generator malfunctions, or battery backups running low. This ensures uninterrupted operation of life-support systems and essential equipment.

5. Coordination of Response via Centralized Monitoring

Alarm systems in hospitals do not operate in isolation; they are integrated into centralized monitoring and communication platforms that coordinate emergency responses efficiently.

Centralized Alarm Management Systems

Modern hospitals utilize centralized alarm management consoles staffed 24/7 by trained personnel. These consoles receive real-time alerts from fire, medical, security, and equipment monitoring systems, prioritize incidents, and dispatch appropriate response teams instantly.

Role in Incident Command and Communication

Centralized systems facilitate communication between various hospital departments, emergency responders, and external agencies. By providing clear, consolidated information about alarm activations and their locations, they streamline decision-making and resource allocation during crises.

Reducing Response Times and Errors

The centralized approach reduces delays and errors that might arise from fragmented alarms or unclear communication. It also enables tracking and logging of all alarm events for post-incident analysis, helping hospitals improve protocols and prevent future incidents.

6. Enhancing Overall Hospital Safety Culture

Alarm systems contribute significantly to cultivating a culture of safety and preparedness within hospital environments.

Promoting Awareness and Readiness

Regular testing, maintenance, and training related to alarm systems keep hospital staff aware of potential risks and their roles in emergency response. This preparedness reduces panic, confusion, and errors during actual emergencies.

Building Patient and Visitor Confidence

Visible alarm systems and well-coordinated responses reassure patients and visitors that the hospital is vigilant and ready to protect their health and safety. This trust is vital for patient satisfaction and institutional reputation.

Compliance with Regulatory and Accreditation Standards

Alarm systems help hospitals meet national and international safety standards such as those mandated by the National Accreditation Board for Hospitals & Healthcare Providers (NABH), Joint Commission

International (JCI), and local fire and safety codes. Compliance is crucial for legal operation, funding, and public confidence.

Types of Alarm Systems in Hospitals

Hospitals operate in highly complex environments where safety, security, and patient care depend on rapid and effective response to emergencies. Alarm systems are essential tools that facilitate early detection, communication, and coordinated action in various critical situations. These systems are broadly categorized based on the type of emergency or monitoring function they address. Below is a detailed overview of the main types of alarm systems used in hospitals:

1. Fire Alarm Systems

Fire alarm systems are among the most crucial safety infrastructures in hospitals, designed to provide early warning in the event of fire or smoke, thus protecting patients, staff, and property.

Components and Functionality

- **Smoke and Heat Detectors:**
  These are strategically placed throughout the hospital, including patient rooms, corridors, operating theaters, storage areas, and utility rooms. Smoke detectors sense particulate matter in the air indicative of fire, while heat detectors respond to rapid increases in temperature or sustained high heat. Together, they ensure early detection of fire even before flames become visible.
- **Manual Pull Stations:**
  In addition to automatic sensors, manual pull stations are installed near exits and in accessible locations so that staff or visitors can manually trigger the alarm upon seeing fire or smoke. This allows human intervention to initiate alerts if the automatic system has not yet detected the hazard.
- **Central Control Panel:**
  All detectors and manual stations feed into a central fire alarm control panel. This panel continuously monitors sensor status and coordinates activation of alarms and other fire safety measures. It also often interfaces with the building's fire suppression systems and emergency lighting.
- **Alarm Notification Devices:**
  Audible alarms such as sirens, bells, and voice evacuation messages, coupled with visual signals like flashing strobe lights, alert all occupants. These signals are designed to be loud and visible enough to awaken or notify even sleeping patients and those in noisy environments.
- **Integration with Sprinkler Systems:**
  Modern fire alarm systems are integrated with automatic sprinkler systems. When smoke or heat is detected, sprinklers activate in affected zones to suppress or extinguish fires, limiting damage and providing additional time for evacuation.

Importance in Hospitals

Due to the presence of oxygen-rich environments, flammable chemicals, and patients unable to evacuate independently, fire alarm systems in hospitals are critical. Early detection and prompt notification reduce risks of injury, fatalities, and infrastructure loss, enabling safe evacuation and firefighting operations.

2. Medical Emergency Alarm Systems

Medical emergencies require immediate response to prevent deterioration or death. Specialized alarm systems alert medical teams instantly, ensuring rapid intervention.

Key Types of Medical Alarms

- **Code Blue Alarms:**
  These alarms are activated when a patient experiences cardiac arrest, respiratory failure, or other life-threatening conditions. The system immediately alerts resuscitation teams, including doctors, nurses, and technicians trained to provide emergency life support. Code Blue alarms are often accompanied by overhead announcements or dedicated alert lights in critical care areas.
- **Nurse Call Systems:**
  These allow patients to request assistance conveniently. Patients can press bedside call buttons, pull cords, or use wireless devices to alert nursing staff for help with medication, mobility, pain, or emergencies. The system sends signals to nursing stations or staff pagers, ensuring timely attention to patient needs.
- **Fall Detection Alarms:**
  Particularly important for elderly or high-risk patients, these sensors monitor patient movement and detect falls or abnormal activity patterns. They use pressure mats, accelerometers, or motion sensors to identify incidents and immediately notify caregivers, minimizing delays in assistance and reducing complications from falls.

Impact on Patient Care

Medical emergency alarms enhance patient safety by reducing response times and preventing adverse events. They empower patients to communicate needs and alert staff to critical conditions, improving overall clinical outcomes and patient satisfaction.

3. Security Alarm Systems

Hospitals must safeguard patients, staff, confidential information, and expensive medical assets. Security alarm systems help detect and deter unauthorized access and security threats.

Components and Applications

- **Intrusion Alarms:**
  These systems monitor restricted areas such as pharmacies, laboratories, data centers, and administrative offices. Sensors include motion detectors, magnetic contacts on doors and windows, and glass break detectors. If unauthorized entry or tampering is detected, alarms activate and notify hospital security teams.
- **Panic Alarms:**
  Staff members, especially those working alone or in high-risk areas, carry or wear panic buttons. These can be pressed discreetly during an emergency (such as assault, medical crisis, or security threat) to summon immediate assistance from security personnel.
- **Perimeter Alarms:**
  These monitor hospital grounds, fences, parking lots, and entrances for breaches. They can include motion sensors, infrared beams, and cameras integrated with alarm triggers to detect and deter intruders before they reach critical hospital buildings.

Importance for Hospital Security

Security alarms protect vulnerable populations (such as psychiatric patients, children, or high-profile individuals) and prevent theft or sabotage of medications and equipment. They ensure a safe working environment for healthcare workers and maintain confidentiality and operational integrity.

4. Environmental Alarm Systems

Hospitals rely on stable environmental conditions and properly functioning equipment to deliver safe care. Environmental alarms monitor potential hazards that could disrupt operations or endanger lives.

Types and Uses

- **Gas Leak Detectors:**
  Hospitals store and use various gases such as oxygen, nitrous oxide, and anesthetics. Gas leak detectors sense dangerous concentrations of flammable or toxic gases, triggering alarms to prompt evacuation or remediation before explosions, poisoning, or fires occur.
- **Temperature and Humidity Alarms:**
  Certain medical equipment, vaccines, pharmaceuticals, and laboratory samples require storage within strict temperature and humidity ranges. Sensors continuously monitor these parameters, activating alarms if conditions fall outside safe limits. This helps prevent spoilage, contamination, and loss of critical medical supplies.
- **Power Failure Alarms:**
  Electrical outages can severely disrupt hospital functions, particularly in ICUs, operating rooms, and emergency departments. Alarm systems monitor power supplies and backup generators, notifying technical staff immediately if failures occur. This ensures quick restoration of power or activation of backup systems, maintaining life-saving equipment function without interruption.

Significance in Hospital Operations

By detecting environmental hazards early, these alarms minimize risks to patient safety and hospital assets. They allow preemptive action to avoid equipment failure, medication loss, and unsafe conditions.

Hospitals employ a diverse range of alarm systems tailored to their unique challenges in fire safety, medical emergencies, security, and environmental control. Each system plays a vital role in safeguarding human life, ensuring operational continuity, and protecting valuable assets. Fire alarm systems provide critical early warnings to prevent devastating losses, while medical emergency alarms enable rapid intervention during patient crises. Security alarms maintain safe premises and protect sensitive areas from unauthorized access. Environmental alarms safeguard critical infrastructure and materials by monitoring conditions that could compromise safety or quality of care.

The integration of these alarm systems with centralized monitoring and communication platforms enhances hospital preparedness and response capabilities. Effective alarm systems are fundamental to creating safe, secure, and resilient healthcare environments where patients receive timely, high-quality care.

Components of Hospital Alarm Systems

Hospitals rely on complex alarm systems to promptly detect emergencies and ensure the safety of patients, staff, and visitors. These systems are composed of several interrelated components that work together to monitor conditions, alert personnel, and facilitate rapid response. Understanding each component's function is essential to designing, operating, and maintaining an effective alarm system.

1. Sensors and Detectors

Sensors and detectors are the frontline devices that continuously monitor the hospital environment for specific changes or abnormalities indicating potential hazards.

- **Types of Sensors:**
    - **Smoke Detectors:** Sense the presence of smoke particles, indicating fire at an early stage.
    - **Heat Detectors:** Trigger alarms when temperatures rise sharply, useful in areas where smoke detection may be impractical.
    - **Motion Detectors:** Detect unauthorized movement in restricted zones or during off-hours, enhancing security.
    - **Gas Detectors:** Monitor concentrations of flammable or toxic gases like oxygen, anesthetic gases, or carbon monoxide.
    - **Sound Detectors:** Can be used to identify distress sounds or alarms from medical equipment.
- **Function:**
  Sensors convert physical or chemical changes in the environment into electrical signals. These signals are then transmitted to control panels for processing. Reliable sensors are calibrated to minimize false alarms while ensuring rapid detection of real threats.
- **Placement and Coverage:**
  Proper placement of sensors is critical. For example, smoke detectors are installed in patient rooms, corridors, and storage areas, while motion sensors are placed at entrances, restricted access points, and parking areas. The coverage area of each sensor is carefully planned to avoid blind spots.

2. Control Panels

The control panel acts as the central nervous system of the alarm system, receiving and interpreting signals from all connected sensors and managing the system's response.

- **Signal Processing:**
  Upon receiving input from sensors, the control panel analyzes the data to determine whether conditions warrant an alarm. It can filter out false positives caused by environmental factors like dust or steam.
- **Decision Making:**
  Advanced control panels have programmable logic to trigger different types of alarms or notifications depending on the nature and location of the detected hazard. For example, a fire detected in the kitchen might initiate a different protocol than a gas leak in a laboratory.
- **Integration:**
  Control panels integrate multiple alarm subsystems, such as fire detection, medical emergency calls, and security alarms, into a single interface. This unified control facilitates coordinated responses and simplifies monitoring.
- **User Interface:**

  Panels include display screens and input controls allowing authorized personnel to view system status, silence false alarms, reset devices, and perform diagnostics.

3. Notification Devices

Notification devices ensure that alarms are communicated clearly and promptly to all relevant individuals, enabling immediate awareness and action.

- **Audible Alarms:**

Sirens, buzzers, horns, and voice annunciators produce loud sounds designed to penetrate ambient noise levels and alert occupants. Different tones or voice messages can indicate the type of emergency (fire, medical, security).

- **Visual Alarms:**
Flashing strobe lights, LED panels, and indicator lights serve to alert hearing-impaired individuals and provide clear signals in noisy or large spaces. Visual alarms are also vital in areas where silence is required, such as operating rooms.
- **Digital Displays and Paging:**
Some systems include text or graphical displays that provide detailed information about the alarm's nature and location. Integration with hospital paging or public address systems enables targeted announcements to specific departments or zones.

4. Communication Interfaces

Communication interfaces connect the alarm system to external communication channels and devices, extending alert reach and enabling coordinated emergency responses.

- **Paging Systems:**
When an alarm activates, the system can send automated messages to pagers or smartphones carried by staff, ensuring rapid mobilization of response teams.
- **Telephony Integration:**
Alarm systems can dial pre-programmed phone numbers, such as security desks, fire departments, or emergency medical teams, to notify them automatically.
- **Mobile and Web Access:**
Modern systems offer secure remote access via mobile apps or web portals, allowing authorized personnel to monitor alarm status, receive alerts, and respond from any location.
- **Security Control Centers:**
Communication interfaces link the alarm system to centralized security operations centers, enabling real-time monitoring, recording, and dispatching of emergency services.

5. Backup Power Supply

Hospitals must ensure alarm systems remain operational at all times, including during power failures or electrical disturbances.

- **Uninterruptible Power Supply (UPS):**
Battery-based UPS units provide immediate backup power to maintain alarm system functionality during short outages or power fluctuations.
- **Generators:**
For extended outages, hospitals use diesel or gas generators that automatically start to supply continuous power to critical systems, including alarms, life-support equipment, and lighting.
- **Battery Maintenance:**
Regular testing and maintenance of batteries and generators are essential to guarantee reliability when needed.
- **Redundancy:**
Alarm systems often incorporate redundant power sources and failover mechanisms to prevent any single point of failure from disabling the system.

The effectiveness of hospital alarm systems depends on the seamless integration of multiple components working in harmony:

- **Sensors and detectors** constantly observe the environment for signs of fire, security breaches, medical emergencies, or environmental hazards.

- **Control panels** act as command centers, processing data and initiating appropriate alarm responses.
- **Notification devices** communicate alerts through sound, light, and digital messages to ensure everyone is promptly informed.
- **Communication interfaces** extend alerts beyond the hospital premises, enabling rapid coordination with emergency responders and internal teams.
- **Backup power supplies** guarantee continuous operation, safeguarding against interruptions that could jeopardize patient and staff safety.

Together, these components create a reliable, responsive alarm infrastructure essential for hospital safety, security, and operational continuity.

Features of an Effective Alarm System in Hospitals

- **Reliability:** Alarms must operate without fail 24/7 and be resistant to false triggers.
- **Immediate Notification:** Alerts must reach appropriate personnel instantly to prompt action.
- **Clear Identification:** Alarms should specify the nature and location of the emergency.
- **Integration:** Systems should work together—fire alarms linked with evacuation systems, medical alarms connected to rapid response teams.
- **User-Friendly Interface:** Easy to understand and operate by all hospital staff, including non-technical users.
- **Regular Testing and Maintenance:** To ensure functionality and compliance with safety standards.
- **Compliance:** Adherence to local and international standards such as NFPA (National Fire Protection Association) codes or hospital accreditation requirements.

Challenges and Considerations

- **Minimizing False Alarms:** Frequent false alarms can cause alarm fatigue, where staff become desensitized and respond slower or ignore alarms. Regular maintenance and proper sensor placement help reduce this.
- **Patient Comfort:** Alarm sounds and lights must balance urgency with minimizing stress for patients, especially in sensitive areas like ICUs.
- **Training:** Staff need comprehensive training on alarm response protocols, interpretation, and operation of alarm systems.
- **System Scalability:** Hospitals must choose systems that can be expanded or upgraded as the facility grows or technology advances.

Alarm systems in hospitals are vital tools that ensure early detection of emergencies, facilitate quick and coordinated responses, and protect lives and property. Their design and implementation require a strategic balance between sensitivity and reliability, user-friendliness, and compliance with safety regulations. Ongoing maintenance, staff training, and integration with other safety systems maximize the effectiveness of hospital alarm systems, making them indispensable for modern healthcare facility management.

Safety Rules in Hospitals

Hospitals are complex environments with a diverse range of hazards including biological risks, chemical exposure, physical injuries, electrical dangers, fire risks, and patient safety concerns. Implementing and adhering to comprehensive safety rules is essential to protect everyone within the facility and maintain smooth hospital operations. Safety rules create a culture of awareness, responsibility, and precaution that reduces accidents, injuries, and legal liabilities.

1. General Safety Rules

- **Maintain Cleanliness:** Always keep floors, corridors, and working areas clean and dry to prevent slips, trips, and falls.
- **Obey Signage:** Follow all posted safety signs, including "No Smoking," "Wet Floor," "Authorized Personnel Only," and emergency exit signs.
- **Use Personal Protective Equipment (PPE):** Wear appropriate PPE such as gloves, masks, gowns, and eye protection as required, especially in infection-prone areas.
- **Report Hazards:** Immediately notify supervisors or safety officers about any unsafe conditions like spills, faulty equipment, or broken fixtures.
- **No Unauthorized Access:** Restrict entry to sensitive areas such as operating rooms, intensive care units, and laboratories to authorized personnel only.
- **Keep Emergency Exits Clear:** Ensure that all fire exits, staircases, and evacuation routes are unobstructed at all times.
- **Proper Waste Disposal:** Follow strict protocols for disposing of biomedical, chemical, and general waste in designated containers.
- **Safe Lifting Techniques:** Use proper posture and assistance tools to avoid back injuries when lifting patients or heavy equipment.

2. Fire Safety Rules

- **Know Fire Exits and Routes:** Familiarize yourself with all emergency exits and evacuation routes within the hospital.
- **No Smoking:** Smoking is prohibited inside the hospital premises to prevent fire hazards.
- **Fire Extinguisher Use:** Only trained personnel should use fire extinguishers; know the location of the nearest extinguisher.
- **Avoid Overloading Electrical Outlets:** Excessive use of plugs or extension cords can cause electrical fires.
- **Report Fire Hazards:** Immediately report any electrical sparks, gas leaks, or smoke sightings to the safety department.
- **Participate in Fire Drills:** Engage actively in fire evacuation drills to understand your role during emergencies.

3. Infection Control Safety Rules

- **Hand Hygiene:** Wash hands thoroughly with soap or use alcohol-based sanitizers before and after patient contact.
- **Use of PPE:** Always wear gloves, masks, gowns, and eye protection when handling infectious materials.
- **Sterilization:** Ensure all medical instruments are sterilized before use.
- **Isolation Procedures:** Follow protocols for isolating patients with contagious diseases to prevent cross-infection.
- **Sharps Handling:** Dispose of needles, scalpels, and other sharps immediately in puncture-proof containers.
- **Vaccination:** Healthcare workers should stay up-to-date with recommended vaccinations (e.g., Hepatitis B, influenza).
- **Safe Handling of Biological Waste:** Segregate and dispose of biological waste following regulatory guidelines.

4. Electrical Safety Rules

- **Inspect Equipment Regularly:** Check electrical devices for frayed cords, exposed wires, or malfunctioning plugs before use.
- **Use Grounded Outlets:** Only plug sensitive medical equipment into grounded sockets to prevent shocks.
- **Do Not Overload Circuits:** Avoid using multiple high-power devices on the same circuit.
- **Turn Off Equipment:** Switch off electrical devices when not in use or before maintenance.
- **Avoid Water Contact:** Keep electrical devices and cords away from wet areas to prevent electrocution.
- **Report Electrical Faults:** Immediately report any sparks, shocks, or unusual odors from electrical devices.

5. Patient Safety Rules

- **Patient Identification:** Always verify patient identity before administering medication, treatment, or procedures.
- **Safe Medication Practices:** Follow prescribed dosages and double-check medications to avoid errors.
- **Use Restraints Judiciously:** Apply physical or chemical restraints only when necessary and with proper authorization.
- **Monitor Equipment:** Regularly check ventilators, infusion pumps, monitors, and other devices to ensure correct functioning.
- **Fall Prevention:** Use bed rails, non-slip mats, and assistive devices for patients at risk of falling.
- **Communicate Clearly:** Ensure accurate and timely communication between healthcare teams during handoffs.

6. Chemical Safety Rules

- **Proper Labeling:** Ensure all chemicals and medications are clearly labeled with contents and hazard warnings.
- **Safe Storage:** Store chemicals in designated, ventilated areas away from heat sources.
- **Use PPE:** Wear gloves, masks, and eye protection when handling hazardous chemicals.
- **Spill Management:** Follow hospital protocols to contain and clean chemical spills safely.
- **Disposal:** Dispose of chemical waste in accordance with environmental regulations and hospital policies.

7. Emergency Safety Rules

- **Know Emergency Numbers:** Keep a list of emergency contact numbers for fire, security, medical emergencies, and maintenance.
- **Emergency Equipment:** Familiarize yourself with the location of first aid kits, defibrillators, and emergency carts.
- **Evacuation Procedures:** Understand and follow the hospital's evacuation plan in case of fire, earthquake, or other disasters.
- **Stay Calm:** In emergencies, maintain composure and follow instructions from designated safety officers.

8. Workplace Safety and Ergonomics

- **Safe Work Practices:** Follow standard operating procedures for all clinical and non-clinical tasks.

- **Ergonomic Design:** Use adjustable chairs, correct monitor heights, and proper lighting to reduce strain.
- **Avoid Fatigue:** Take breaks and avoid long shifts without rest to reduce accidents caused by fatigue.
- **Use Mechanical Aids:** Employ wheelchairs, trolleys, and lifting devices instead of manual handling whenever possible.

Hospital safety rules are comprehensive guidelines designed to create a secure, hazard-free environment for patients, healthcare workers, and visitors. Strict adherence to these rules minimizes the risk of accidents, infections, and injuries, thereby enhancing the overall quality of healthcare delivery. Ongoing training, awareness programs, and enforcement of safety protocols ensure a proactive safety culture that safeguards lives and upholds hospital integrity.

Questionaire

UNIT I: Overview of Hospital Administration

1. Define hospital administration.
2. What distinguishes a hospital from an industry?
3. Name two types of hospitals based on ownership.
4. List three challenges faced in hospital administration.
5. What is hospital planning?
6. Why is equipment planning important in hospitals?
7. Define functional planning in hospital administration.
8. What are the key components of hospital planning?
9. Explain the term 'hospital infrastructure'.
10. Mention two factors considered in hospital layout planning.
11. What is the role of management in hospital planning?
12. Define patient flow in hospital planning.
13. How does technology affect hospital administration?
14. What is the significance of regulatory compliance in hospitals?
15. Explain the difference between inpatient and outpatient services.
16. What role does financial planning play in hospital administration?
17. Name two types of hospital services.
18. Define 'healthcare delivery system'.
19. What is meant by 'hospital capacity planning'?
20. State one advantage of functional planning in hospitals.

UNIT II: Human Resource Management in Hospital

1. Define Human Resource Management (HRM).
2. State any three principles of HRM.
3. List four functions of HRM.
4. What is the role of the HRD manager in a hospital?
5. Define Human Resource Inventory.
6. Explain manpower planning.
7. Why is recruitment important in HRM?
8. What does staff development mean?
9. Define 'job analysis' in the context of HRM.
10. What is the significance of training in hospitals?
11. Mention two types of manpower forecasting methods.
12. What is performance appraisal?
13. Define employee retention.
14. What is motivation in HRM?
15. Explain the importance of employee welfare.
16. What is the role of communication in HRM?
17. Define 'succession planning'.
18. What is the difference between recruitment and selection?
19. What are the qualities of a good HR manager?
20. Define 'job description' and 'job specification'.

UNIT III: Recruitment and Training

1. Name five departments commonly found in a hospital.
2. Define recruitment.
3. What is the purpose of the selection process?
4. Mention two types of recruitment sources.
5. Define induction training.
6. What is on-the-job training?
7. Mention two methods of off-the-job training.
8. Explain the term 'training evaluation'.
9. What is leadership grooming?
10. Define promotion in hospital administration.
11. What is the purpose of employee transfer?
12. Name two factors influencing recruitment.
13. What is meant by 'training guidelines'?
14. What is the significance of employee orientation?
15. Define 'probation period'.
16. What is mentoring in training?
17. Mention two advantages of training for hospital staff.
18. What is meant by 'employee turnover'?
19. Define 'career development'.
20. What is the importance of succession planning in leadership?

UNIT IV: Supportive Services

1. What is the Medical Records Department?
2. Define Central Sterilization and Supply Department (CSSD).
3. Mention two functions of the hospital pharmacy.
4. What is the importance of food services in a hospital?
5. What is the role of laundry services in hospitals?
6. Define biomedical waste management.
7. Name two types of hospital supportive services.
8. What is inventory management in pharmacy?
9. Explain the function of sterilization in CSSD.
10. What role do medical records play in patient care?
11. Mention two challenges faced by supportive services.
12. Define patient dietetics.
13. What is the role of transport services in hospitals?
14. Mention two safety precautions in laundry services.
15. Explain the significance of packaging in pharmacy services.
16. What is the role of dietary planning in food services?
17. Define cold chain management in pharmacy.
18. What is the purpose of maintaining medical records?
19. Mention one technological advancement used in supportive services.
20. What is the role of housekeeping in hospital supportive services?

UNIT V: Communication and Safety Aspects in Hospital

1. What is communication planning?
2. Name four modes of communication used in hospitals.
3. Define verbal communication.
4. What is non-verbal communication?
5. Explain the purpose of telephone communication in hospitals.
6. What is ISDN?
7. Define public address system in hospital context.
8. What is piped music communication?
9. Mention two benefits of CCTV in hospitals.
10. What is loss prevention in hospitals?
11. State two fire safety measures in hospitals.
12. What is the function of an alarm system in hospitals?
13. Define safety rules in hospital administration.
14. What is meant by 'emergency communication'?
15. Mention two advantages of electronic communication in hospitals.
16. What is the role of security personnel in hospitals?
17. Explain the term 'alarm fatigue'.
18. Name two safety devices used in hospitals.
19. What is the importance of regular fire drills?
20. Define 'confidentiality' in hospital communication.

Epilogue

The study of Hospital Administration provides a comprehensive understanding of the strategic, operational, and clinical frameworks essential to manage modern healthcare institutions effectively. This syllabus, structured across five essential units, equips students with a multidimensional perspective of hospital operations and the critical roles they play in delivering quality patient care.

Beginning with an overview of hospital administration, learners are introduced to the foundational differences between hospitals and industries, key planning methods, and the unique challenges faced in a healthcare setting. The concepts of hospital, equipment, and functional planning form the strategic core that guides every hospital's development and service delivery approach.

The second unit, focusing on Human Resource Management, emphasizes the importance of managing the most vital asset of any hospital—its people. Students explore the principles and functions of HRM, the responsibilities of HRD managers, and the systematic approach to workforce planning through human resource inventories and manpower forecasting.

Recruitment and Training, covered in the third unit, delve into the practical aspects of sourcing, selecting, and nurturing healthcare professionals. It highlights not only the structural setup of various hospital departments but also the significance of developing future leaders through leadership grooming, well-defined promotion policies, and transparent transfer systems.

The fourth unit on Supportive Services emphasizes departments that function behind the scenes yet are integral to hospital efficiency. From medical records to sterilization, pharmacy, food, and laundry services—students learn how these functions support core clinical care and uphold the standards of hygiene, nutrition, medication safety, and administrative order.

Finally, the study culminates with Communication and Safety Aspects, spotlighting the crucial role of effective information exchange and preventive systems in a hospital environment. Learners gain insights into verbal, non-verbal, and electronic communication, the use of systems like ISDN and CCTV, and critical areas such as loss prevention, fire safety, and compliance with hospital safety protocols.

In conclusion, this syllabus fosters a holistic view of hospital administration, preparing students to become efficient healthcare administrators who can balance operational excellence, human capital management, and patient-centric care. It encourages future professionals to uphold ethics, ensure patient safety, and drive innovation in healthcare delivery.